Sandra,
God's best to
you! I look forward
to more talks!
In Him,
Ren Vandesteeg
Ch, Col (Ret) USAF

WHEN DUTY CALLS

A Guide to Equip Active Duty, Guard and Reserve Personnel
and Their Loved Ones for Military Separations

To: Sandra
Carol Vandesteeg
Proverbs 3:5+6

WHEN DUTY CALLS

CALLS

A Guide to Equip Active Duty, Guard and Reserve Personnel
and Their Loved Ones for Military Separations

**CAROL
VANDESTEEG**

Revised
& Expanded

WINEPRESS WP PUBLISHING

Packaged by WinePress Publishing, PO Box 428, Enumclaw, WA 98022. The views expressed or implied in this work do not necessarily reflect those of WinePress Publishing. The author is ultimately responsible for the design, content, and editorial accuracy of this work.

The military emblems on the cover are used by permission from each branch of the armed services. Their use does not imply endorsement of this book by any military branch.

Unless otherwise noted, all Scriptures are taken from the Holy Bible, New International Version, Copyright © 1973, 1978, 1984 by the International Bible Society. Used by permission of Zondervan Publishing House. The "NIV" and "New International Version" trademarks are registered in the United States Patent and Trademark Office by International Bible Society.

ISBN 1-57921-376-6
Library of Congress Catalog Card Number: 2001088454

To the One who
prepared and equipped me.

CONTENTS

Contents

Contents

PREFACE

In the uncertain political climate of our world today, readiness is foremost on the minds of a large number of our military personnel and their families. If they haven't thought about it already, now is certainly the time to begin! The demands of America's military mission are more intense than in recent years, as servicemen and women deploy to locations around the world. Active Duty personnel cannot accomplish the mission alone; Guard and Reserve personnel in increasing numbers are mobilized/activated to contribute to the mission on a full-time basis instead of the part-time contributions they've previously made. Reserve and Guard members may not know how or where to begin to prepare themselves and their loved ones for deployment. Some Active Duty families haven't given readiness much thought either.

I've been privileged to speak about preparation for deployment at military installations in the continental United States, Alaska, and overseas in Germany, and find that families *are* concerned about whether they're equipped to deal with the stress and uncertainty that result when a loved one is deployed. It's normal to wonder how you'll handle family separation, and to have concerns about one another's safety and well-being while you'll be apart. I know first-hand how that feels. My husband, Ren, is on Active Duty in the Air Force. We've lived through TDYs and deployments, and continue to be vulnerable to family separation.

Our most dramatic family separation was Ren's deployment to Operation Desert Shield/Storm in 1990, on only two hours' notice. The Air Force had little to offer family members to prepare them for deployments back then. Now military installations in each component of the Armed Forces have programs or resources to help families during duty-imposed separations from their military sponsors. However, information can be difficult for family members to find, and not everyone is comfortable attending the pre-deployment meetings that are held. Sometimes the resources are given to the military member, who is expected to share them with his or her family, but the resources don't always make the trip home or find their way into the families' hands. *When Duty Calls* helps bridge that gap. In fact, a number of military units now use this book to help their personnel prepare for deployments, as well as reunion after the deployments.

When Duty Calls helps military members and their loved ones discover ways to prepare for and equip themselves for times of family separation. I wrote this guide from the perspective of the traditional two-parent family in which the male is the service member, because that is my experience. I recognize that the military includes male and female members, married and single, as well as dual-military career couples and single parents, and I address each in this book. Where there are references to the military member as the male or father, I do not mean to exclude females or mothers. The terminology I use reflects my experience, not any bias. I support and am proud of all of our military members, and feel indebted to them for their service on behalf of our country.

If you're a military family member who doesn't feel comfortable attending the support group meeting around you, or using the military resources available to you, I hope reading this book will give you the confidence you need to get more involved in your military community. Please use the facilities and benefits that are offered to you. You don't have to get through deployments all by yourself! This book will help you find out what the military offers to you, and will give you ideas that you can apply to your family's need as you face family separation. If you are civilian, *When Duty Calls* will help you understand loved ones or friends who are living with the stress that goes along with the military lifestyle.

Carol Vandesteeg
San Antonio, Texas

ACKNOWLEDGMENTS

I acknowledge, with gratitude, each person at WinePress who has had a part in the production of and presentation of this book to the reader. Athena, Gloria, Lisa, Tim, and the rest of the staff, thanks! As in previous editions, I also recognize Colonel (Retired) Edward Skender, Nancy Anderson, and Randall Williams for their advice/teaching in years past.

Thank you to those who referred me to resources or made me aware of corrections to be made to earlier editions. A special thanks to those who have shamelessly and generously spread their personal recommendations of my work. You know who you are, Mariel, Chief H., Doc R., Celeste, Ken, and a host of others I can't take time to list. May God bless you for your kindness.

Last, and closest to my heart, thank you, Ren, Mike, and Dan, for your constant and continuing love, encouragement, and support. Thanks to them and extended family members who have shared my joy for this Third Edition of *When Duty Calls*.

I

Preparing for Family Separation

· 1 ·

You're Going
Where? When?

It was August 13, 1990. Like every Monday, I was working at the base hospital pharmacy when, unexpectedly, my husband Ren came hurrying into the building.

"He probably wants to meet me for lunch today," I thought.

As he approached the window, I said, "Hi, sweetie."

"Hi. Is there someone who can take over the window for you? I need to talk to you."

"Right now?"

"Yes. Hurry. I'm going to Saudi Arabia."

"When?"

"Today."

The pharmacist, Major West, said, "Let him in."

The door opened. Ren was soon inside.

"I have to be at the Mobility Center and ready to go by noon. Can you leave now so you can help me pack?"

It was 10 A.M! Someone must have taken my place at the window, but all I heard was the Major saying, "Can they do that?"

I fumbled for my purse, still not believing my ears. "Saudi Arabia." "Today." "Can they do that?" "Noon."

Ren had been in his office, counseling, when Chaplain Jeff Timm opened the door.

"Ren, could you step out into the hallway? I need to talk to you."

"I'm counseling."

"Ren, I have to talk to you *NOW*."

The sudden interruption stunned Ren as he thought, *"Jeff knows better than to violate professional courtesy like this. He's more sensitive than that. What's going on? This better be important."*

Apologizing to the couple in his office, Ren stepped into the hallway.

The door was barely closed when Jeff began to speak. "Ren, you're being deployed to Saudi Arabia."

"When?"

"Today."

"When?"

"Noon."

As he absorbed the shock, Ren thought out loud, "But I'm not even the mobility chaplain."

"You were asked for by name by SAC Headquarters. Maybe they asked for you because you were in Saudi before." (Note: SAC stands for Strategic Air Command.)

As Ren stared at the checklist of personal items he needed to take along, Jeff said, "Just go home and get packed and we'll meet you at the mobility center with the chapel trunk."

When we got home we went down the list and, mechanically, began to fill his duffle bag. I quickly threw a load of his underwear into the washing machine. Would there even be time for it to wash and dry before he had to leave?

Meanwhile, Ren woke Dan up. Our sleepy-eyed 16-year-old son was sent to the Base Exchange (BX) to get some shaving cream and a straight-edged razor for Dad.

"Do you have an extra bottle of shampoo and some deodorant for me to take along?" Ren called from the bedroom.

"I think so." But I didn't find any. "I'll call Dan at the BX and ask him to get that too."

The duffle bag was almost full as the three of us gathered in the kitchen around 11:15 A.M. Ren wanted to call Mike, our oldest son, to say goodbye, but Mike was working on a construction site in California and there was no way to get through to him until evening. (In 1990, people didn't carry cell phones.) With Mike on our minds, we sat at the kitchen table to pray. We brought our confused emotions to God, asking Him to help us sort out our thoughts, and to give each of us strength, protection, and a clear sense of His presence until we would be reunited. We had no idea when that might be.

The mobility center was not very busy. McConnell Air Force Base (AFB) did not deploy many people at a time—mostly weathermen and firemen—and a chaplain and chaplain's assistant.

Dan and I weren't allowed to walk inside with Ren, but decided to wait in the car in case he could come back out before he left. After only a short wait, our patience was rewarded when he ran out with a short message for us.

"It doesn't look like I'm going to Saudi after all, but I can't tell you where I am going. It's classified. Just thought you'd like to know. I'll contact you when I can. I love you both."

After a quick kiss we said the final goodbye and he was gone again. I ached inside as he walked away from the car. Dan and I looked at each other and sat in silence for a moment.

"Now what?"

"Well, we have to be at school by 1:30," my son said. That was Dan's assigned time to register for his junior year of high school.

"Want to go to McDonald's for lunch first?"

"OK."

We didn't talk a lot at lunch or in the line for registration at school. The excitement of the students who were glad to see each other again surrounded us but seemed out of place. Didn't they know this wasn't a happy day?

It may not have been a happy day for us, but it was for them. They were renewing relationships with friends they hadn't seen all summer. Dan and I had to adjust to life without Ren, and trust that eventually we'd feel like laughing again too, even though we didn't feel jovial that day.

After we got home, Dan asked me if we were still going to Michigan. We had been planning to leave on Wednesday to visit relatives in Michigan for two weeks. We looked forward to seeing Grandma and Aunt Dena, who were coming from the Netherlands.

"Yes, Dan, we'll still go. Dad just won't be there with us."

"It doesn't seem fair, does it? The one time his Dutch relatives will be there, he can't come along. He couldn't even say goodbye to Mike!"

After a long pause, we looked at each other and said, in unison, "Life isn't fair."

Ren and I had taught the boys that life doesn't always deliver what we expect and sometimes events that happen may not seem just or right, but we still have to live in those circumstances. We might feel let down when life doesn't seem fair, but that's precisely when we can find grace and strength if we turn to the Lord. So, in our family over the years, "Life isn't fair," eventually became another way to say, "We may not understand, but God does."

God's care got us through the two-hour notification of Ren's deployment and each day of the family separation. We didn't have time to prepare for the time apart—just react to it.

Fortunately, most people have more than two hours of notification when they're deployed.

· 2 ·

ARE YOU READY?

Is family separation part of your military experience? If it isn't yet, get ready, because it will be soon! Family separation is an expected part of the Active Duty military lifestyle. Instead of predictable assignments, unexpected deployments with varying amounts of notification are common. According to the Office of the Secretary of Defense for Reserve Affairs, the same thing is true for those who serve in the Reserves, who make up about half of the total military force.[1] The military has been reduced by about 40% since 1990, yet the number of deployments has increased by about 400%. The reality in today's military is that we should expect longer work hours and more frequent deployments to affect families of every military component.

Each component tries to meet the increased demand efficiently. For example, the Air Force established ten main expeditionary groups to take turns covering deployments, with the goal that military members will deploy only 90 days every 15 months. Air Force Reserve and Air National Guard personnel are included in the rotations. However, although the Air Force goal is one 90-day deployment every 15 months, many military families live with more frequent and longer separations than that projection.

In addition to deployments, Active Duty military members face temporary duty away from home, field exercises, or unaccompanied tours of duty that separate them from their families. Additionally, wives don't always move with their husbands when they get Permanent Change of Station (PCS) orders. Wives may want to pursue their own careers, keep children in the same schools, or need to stay behind to sell houses. So families may live in two separate locations. Sometimes that choice is preferable to uprooting families, and more military couples make the sacrifice of living apart now than have in the past. These separations, like deployments, require preparation and adjustment and must be planned for carefully.

FAMILY SEPARATION AND STRESS

Even when family separation is expected, it is not routine and each separation is unique. Researchers say that the most severe stress a military wife and children face is forced separation from the father.[2] That stress can be minimized by preparation. Part of preparation is believing you will successfully deal with the challenge. Captain Stan Beach, a Retired Navy Chaplain, said, "When family separations come, we aren't suddenly sprinkled with stardust from heaven. We either have the right stuff, or we don't."[3] You can decrease your need for stardust from heaven by beginning to prepare yourself now for the inevitable deployment or mobilization.

If your husband came home today to tell you he was about to deploy or be mobilized, how would you feel? Wives who are new to the military may feel like they've already lost the closeness of their relationships with their mothers, relatives, and friends, and now the only person close to them, their husbands, will leave them alone in a new environment. Other women may have established relationships in their military or civilian communities that they know they can rely on when their husbands are gone. They may feel ready for the challenge of the separation. Some wives have such mixed emotions when they get news of deployment that they don't know *what* they're feeling. They may forget that their husbands also feel stress when they are deployed.

Many military servicemen and women feel stress because they want to do their jobs well and care for their families too. The demands of deployment or mobilization seem to make them have to choose between family and career. They don't look forward to telling their families that they have to be separated because of military duty. When Sgt. Patrick Dawson deployed from Fort Hood in support of the War on Terrorism, he said, "It's hard to leave your family. It's the hardest part of my job, I reckon."[4]

Staff Sergeant Daniel Diaz-Centeno agrees. He said, "There's never going to be enough practice to where you get used to being away from your family."[5] It's hard to leave your family to go to war, on a peacekeeping mission, on a humanitarian mission, on a Navy cruise, or on temporary duty assignment.

EXPECTING SEPARATIONS

When you volunteer to join any component of the military, you and your family must accept the fact that you could be called to go to war. Active Duty, Guard, and Reserve families may have to consciously remind themselves that their military spouses could be called away. Thinking of separation as an inevitable part of Active Duty, Reserve, or Guard life gives families better attitudes when they face deployment or mobilization.

Whatever the reason for the family separation, the ability of the family to communicate freely and carry on daily routines is interrupted. Interruption may make adjustments necessary, but problems and adjustments don't have to be seen as bad. They may not be pleasant or be our choice, but we can endure them, and emerge better than we were before.

TRAIN YOUR FAMILY

The attitudes of parents set the tone for how children respond to separations, and children often mimic the behavior patterns or attitudes toward separation they see in their parents. For this reason, if there is enough advance notification, husbands should tell their wives about deployment or mobilization in private so they have time to talk and get used to the idea before they tell the children. Then, when the time is right, the parents can have a positive attitude about what is ahead as they give the news to their children. When everyone in the family gets used to the reality of the deployment, the family can take steps to prepare for the time apart.

As you think about how to prepare your family for a military separation, it may help to think of the military's training system as a model to follow. The first thing a person does after enlisting in the military is go to basic training to learn how to work and survive in the military environment. The family needs basic training[6] to handle the military lifestyle too. Active Duty, Reserve, and Guard members and their families all need to know how the system works and what it has to offer them. Spouses need to be self-reliant enough to take care of family business if that becomes necessary. They need to be aware of the fact that "At times like this it may seem the service is coming before the family. It is. It has to. It won't work any other way. . . . You can send him away complaining or send him away with a kiss. Either way, he has to go."[7] Expect separation as part of family life rather than a traumatic interruption.

Valorie Torbert and her two sons hugged Sgt. First Class Kenneth Torbert goodbye, and as he departed she said, "We just do what we've got to do with the belief that they're coming back real soon. I'm glad he's going; he's going for all the right reasons. This is his job. I knew that when I married him."[8] Valorie's good attitude must have made it easier for her husband to leave, and provided a positive perspective on family separation for herself and their sons. She knew they would survive the deployment and was ready to face it. You can decide to have the same perspective toward your deployments!

1. AP. "Military reserves to become more important, defense official says,"
    Minot Daily News. 11 January 1999; A-7.

2. Schumm, Walter, and D. Bruce Bell and Giao Tran. "Family Adaptation to
    the Demands of Army Life: A Review of Findings." U. S. Army Research
    Institute for the Behavioral and Social Sciences: January 1994; 13.

3. Beach, Captain Stan J., Chaplain, U. S. Navy (Retired). "Enduring and
    Prospering in Your Military Calling," in *Deployed, Not Disconnected: Hope
    and Help For Husbands and Wives Facing Separations Due to Military As-
    signments,* ed. Don and Karen Martin: (Englewood, CO: Officer's Christian
    Fellowship, 1991), 3.

4. Christenson, Sig. "Families say goodbyes at Fort Hood," *San Antonio Ex-
    press-News*. 15 January 2003; A-5.

5. Zowie, Richard. "12th TRANS mechanic reflects on deployment," Wing-
    spread. 10 January 2003; 4.

6. Cline, Lydia Sloan. *Today's Military Wife: Meeting the Challenges of Service
    Life*. 2nd Edition. (Mechanicsburg, PA: Stackpole Books, 1992), 200.

7. Ibid., 202.

8. Hettena, Seth. AP. "Thousands of GIs ship out for gulf," San Antonio Ex-
    press-News. 7 January 2003; A-4.

· 3 ·

PREPARING SINGLE MILITARY MEMBERS FOR DEPLOYMENT

If you are single and don't have children, you don't have the same concerns as service members that have dependents, but you must still prepare yourself for deployments. You have bank accounts to take care of, bills to pay, and mail, among other concerns. You may want to consider the following questions to be sure you are ready to be deployed:

- How will your bills be paid if you are suddenly deployed? Do you have arrangements to pay your car payment, insurance (auto, health, life, household goods), club membership, credit card payments, department store layaway, Deferred Payment Plan (DPP), and loan payments? Are any of your payments made automatically by allotment? What would happen if you were gone and the allotment was late? Do you have a backup system? If not, how will you avoid late payments and late payment charges?

- When do your car license, inspection, insurance, and installation registration need to be renewed? Who will take care of it if you are gone? Who will take care of your car while you're gone?

- Have you assigned Power of Attorney (POA) to someone to do the specific things you need taken care of?

- Do you need to give someone POA to conduct your banking? Carefully consider who you will give access to your bank account. If the account is listed in your name only, do you have a beneficiary listed on the account?
- Do you have a will? Who will take care of your things if you do not return? You may not own a lot of things, but the decisions about who will get them are yours to make.
- Who will take responsibility for your personal possessions while you are gone?
- How will you file and pay your income taxes while you are gone?
- Do your friends and relatives have your deployment address?
- Do you have someone designated to pick up your mail, or will you have it forwarded to you? You have to fill out a request form if you want the post office to forward your mail. If you ask someone to pick up your mail, he or she will need POA.
- Do your relatives know how to contact you in case of emergency? Do they know how to contact the Red Cross for emergency notification?
- Do your relatives have the names and phone numbers of your First Sergeant and Commander?
- Do your First Sergeant and Commander have your parents' names and phone numbers?
- Do you have pets or plants that will need care while you are gone? Who will take care of them?
- Do you have a second job? If so, does your employer know you will be deployed?
- Do you have a list of things you will need with you on your deployment? Where is your immunization record? Do you have any health records that must be carried with you?
- Do you have a back-up plan for the care of your mail, housing, car, etc., in case the person you designate is unable to follow through on helping while you're gone? Sometimes people designated to help are deployed during the time they are helping someone else.
- Review all of the above every year to be sure it is still effective.

Attend pre-deployment briefings if they are offered in your unit or elsewhere on your installation. Do you have a boyfriend or girl-friend, parents, or other friends or relatives that are close to you that you could invite to the pre-deployment briefing? The information given at this meeting may be important to those who are close to you, and help them feel connected to you after you leave. They will probably be grateful for the opportunity to be introduced to your military lifestyle and to people who will be available to give them information about you after you're gone.

Although most of this book is written for families, you will find a significant amount of information that you can apply to your situation as a single, so I encourage you to read further.

· 4 ·

PREPARING YOUR FAMILY FOR DEPLOYMENT

COMMUNICATE EARLY

Although preparing for deployment does help reduce stress, no amount of preparation can erase it entirely. "But the perception of even some control can be enough to lessen most negative responses and become a base for building positive coping behaviors."[1] Knowing what to expect and open communication about the feelings of all family members are good places to begin to find a perception of control. You may want to set aside an evening or weekend to talk about the possibility of deployment with your family. Tell them that it's likely that you will be deployed, although you don't know when. Talk about what would happen if you were deployed so they will be ready if you are called. Make sure they know that you may be given advance warning or you could be deployed without notice. Ask each member of the family to share his or her concerns and feelings.

When you have advance notice of a family separation, having a series of family meetings during the weeks leading up to the deployment will keep concerns out in the open where they can be addressed. The emotions of family members will probably be strained just before the separation. Many families experience frustration because the deploying family member has to take extra time both at work and at home to prepare for the separation; that can result in longer work hours and less family time when the family wants more time together.

The decrease in the time families have left together can also cause wives to dwell on the deployment, wonder how their families will survive separation, or even doubt that they can survive. As time for the husband's departure approaches, the wife may gradually pull away in order to protect herself from hurt, without even realizing why. The husband may become totally involved with his work just before he leaves. The wife may feel like it's her husband's fault that the family doesn't have more time together before he leaves. Disagreements and tears may become more frequent, children may misbehave more, and little irritants may become major issues. Family members may build walls around themselves to hide the pain of the departure, and that breaks down communication.[2] If reactions like these are recognized as responses to the deployment, they don't have to cause major problems in families.

COMMON CONCERNS

Most families say that deployment hasn't caused serious problems for them. The concerns voiced most often by military members who participated in one survey include the family's safety in the event of war; family's safety in the community; children's health, well-being, and daycare; money to pay bills; and whether the family car and household repairs would be taken care of.[3] Everyone who deploys or mobilizes and leaves loved ones behind has concerns about their family's welfare and how the absence will affect them.

The concerns of every family member are important, and families deal with separations more effectively if each person knows that the rest of the family cares about the issues that are important to him or her. Don't avoid sharing your feelings; make a conscious effort to be open and honest in your communication with each other. A husband may want to tell his family he knows it won't be easy for them when he's gone, but he has confidence in them and knows they'll be OK. He might want to mention things individual members in the family can do to show them how they can solve problems that could come up in his absence.

Preparing for deployment may remind a couple or family that they have not been communicating well and may help them begin to give more attention to communication. *Don't assume anything* if you want your relationship to be strong enough to get through tough times. Talk about concerns or problems as they are brought up by both spouses. For example, recognize that after the husband leaves, social life will be different for the wife because married friends will probably not include her in as many activities as usual, and even if they do she may feel awkward about being alone; she will not feel totally comfortable with single people either. When a wife thinks about that and has the opportunity to talk to her husband about it, she can feel more comfortable about expecting less group social activity during the separation.

See if there are any misunderstandings between husband and wife about what each of you expects during the separation. Try to understand your husband's feelings and how he approaches the deployment. Many wives find that when they talk about their feelings their husbands will share that they find separation difficult too. Wives can discover that their husbands are well trained and prepared to go to war, but they are concerned about the family's welfare in their absence. Husbands can discover what their wives feel insecure or apprehensive about and fortify those areas with moral support.

Some military members are married to spouses whose first language is not English. If that is true in your family, does your spouse speak and understand English well enough to be self-sufficient while you are gone? If her command of the language is limited, ask her whether she wants or needs help with understanding and translation while you are gone. She may be more comfortable if there is someone who knows both languages that she can go to for assistance when she needs it, even if she can communicate sufficiently in English. Sometimes it's just easier to think and speak in a native language during times of stress, so try to make that possible for those whose first language is not English.

If you discuss these things before you're notified of deployment or mobilization, the family will have more time to enjoy each other before the military member leaves, because the issues have been settled. The last days together can be used to reassure each other and show confidence in each other's ability to get through the family separation in spite of hardships that may come.

CONNECT WITH YOUR UNIT

Hardships may seem easier to handle if your family knows they're not alone. Your family may want to try to develop relationships with families of people at work. Many military units deploy as units, so relationships formed with co-workers continue during deployments. The husband will have friends to relate to as he deploys, and the family at home will have relationships with their families. If you don't already know the families of the people you work with or who work with your husband, invite them over for a visit or go on a family outing with them to get acquainted.

If your unit has family days to introduce your family to what you do at work, attend them as a family. The more your family knows and understands about your job and how it fits into the mission of the military, the more they can appreciate the role you play and envision you at work when you are gone. If it's possible, have someone take pictures of you with each family member at your work station. Your family can keep the pictures when you are gone and feel your care and presence when they look at them. A connection between your care for your family and your work will make the separation more bearable for both you and your family.

Some units are creative in their efforts to meet the needs of military family members. For example, McConnell Air Force Base, in Wichita, Kansas, held a mobility line to show family members what the servicemen go through when they deploy. Their program included signing in, a briefing from a unit deployment manager, preventative health assessments, and boarding buses to the mobility center. At the mobility center attendees processed through a line where they were asked to show their ID cards and immunization records, and they learned about the Military Personnel Flight. They met representatives from the same squadrons who are present in real-world mobility lines, and received an intelligence briefing about their simulated deployed location.

The Maryland Air National Guard's 175th Wing held a similar event. Although their Family Deployment Day didn't include waiting in mobility lines, it gave families a good perception of what happens when military members deploy. Family members had the opportunity to see airplanes, work centers, and booths representing organizations that play a role in mobility, such as insurance, legal, pay, and family readiness.

The 176th Wing at Kulis Air National Guard Base, in Anchorage, Alaska, held a weekend readiness conference to introduce family members to their mission and teach them how to prepare for deployments. While the military members performed their drill weekend, family members saw the aircraft, had lunch in the chow hall, and learned about the military structure and benefits. Their briefings included presentations about the commissary, the First Sergeant's role, OPSEC (Operations Security), COMSEC (Communications Security), military pay, family programs, legal, and other military benefits and services, in addition to presentations that addressed preparing for deployments, getting through family separations, and reunion.

If your family has the opportunity, participate in events like those at McConnell Air Force Base, the Maryland Air National Guard, or the Alaska National Guard. The events are usually open to children as well as adults, and provide a learning environment that is a lot of fun. An important part of the learning is the visual image of their loved ones' military duty that these events give families. The visual image and experience help families feel connected to military members when they're away during deployments.

PLAN FOR FAMILY UNITY AND SUPPORT

Help your family find creative ways to maintain closeness during the separation. Ask each family member which methods of long distance communication are most meaningful to him or her and how often he or she'd like to hear from you while you're deployed. Different family members may prefer cassette tape exchanges, photographs, letters—or maybe greeting cards, postcards, videos, encoded messages, or puzzle messages; others may prefer unique stationery, or paintings or drawings by young children or artistic family members. If you know what means something to each family member, you'll be able to communicate with him or her more effectively while you're away. And if you tell them what you'd like to hear about or receive when you're gone, they'll have an opportunity to do the same for you.

Deployment disrupts life and causes pain for everyone in the family. Instead of giving in to the temptation to think conditions are rougher for one person than the others during those times, families should find ways to help and support one another through them. Before you are deployed, whether you are Active Duty, Reserve, or Guard, make sure your family knows there is someone they can call who will help them. It will be most helpful if the person they call knows and understands the military system. If there are pre-deployment briefings offered at your unit or installation, take your family to the meetings. Friends and relatives who are close to you may also benefit from the briefings. These meetings will give your family, parents, and friends a means to feel connected to you while you are gone.

Anything your family can do to build a bridge with the Active Duty, Reserve, and Guard communities will give them less of a feeling of isolation or alienation when the family is separated. Preparation for the inevitable military family separations helps your family appreciate the military lifestyle even during unpleasant times. The Family Service or Support Center at your installation will help you prepare for separations, and you can also do many things to help yourself get ready for deployment.

Remember the reference to the military's training system as a model to prepare families? Comparing the family to the military structure may help service members understand the importance of preparing their families for separation. "As an effective military officer you know the value of training and encouraging a staff, particularly the deputy or executive officer. Your wife is your deputy in the family; she is your 'vice-commander.' When you are separated from your family because of military duties, she must be equipped and motivated to carry on your family training program. How can you help her do this?"[4] Lieutenant Colonel Ward Graham suggests that one way to help prepare the family is to develop a "briefing guide" for their use. His suggestion is a great idea, limited only by your family's imagination. Maybe you'd like to make your own *Family Deployment Guide* (see the *Family Deployment Guide* section of this book for further information).

Whether you include them in a *Family Deployment Guide* or on a separate list, gather important phone numbers that your family may need while you are gone. The list should include the numbers of your First Sergeant, Commander, police, fire department, ambulance, and hospital emergency room. Be sure your family, parents, and in-laws know how to reach you while you are deployed. Do you have an address to give them for correspondence? If there is an emergency and they need to reach you, do they know how to do it? Do they know how the Red Cross is used for emergency notifications and aid?

Be sure your family is able to receive ALL of the information and support your installation offers. One Lieutenant Colonel filled out the pre-deployment questionnaire at his base Family Support Center, and checked "NO" for the "May we contact your family" line of the form. When asked why, he said, "My wife does just fine. . . . She knows about taking care of herself." His wife happened to walk in as he said this, and she was not happy. "What on earth did you say that for? Do you think I can't answer a phone and decide for myself if I want to get involved in a program? . . . Did you know that 90% of you men do this?" As I travel to speak at spouse support groups, readiness workshops, and conferences, I am consistently told that military members forget to ask their spouses for input.

Unfortunately, she was correct in saying that most men decide for their wives that they don't need to be contacted during deployments. Why *wouldn't* a husband want his wife to experience as much support as possible? *Please check "YES" on forms that request permission to contact your spouse when you're deployed!* If your spouse doesn't want to be involved, she will say so, and she won't be bothered with phone calls she doesn't want. But, let *HER* make that decision!

PLAN TO SHARE HOUSEHOLD CHORES

Some families help their children visualize the comparison between the family and the military lifestyle by having a family change of command ceremony before deployments. They prepare a list of responsibilities and chores for each family member. If you like that idea but you aren't sure what household jobs children of different ages are ready for, here are some examples: three-and four-year-olds can put away toys, dust, feed a pet, or empty small wastebaskets; five-and six-year-olds can make their beds, tidy up a room, set the table, make a sandwich, help with cooking and cleaning up afterward, and fold clothes; seven-through nine-year-olds can clean the tub and sink, wash clothes, and vacuum; ten-through twelve-year-olds can wash the car, entertain younger children, fix simple meals, and clean up the house.

You may want to have a family planning meeting to draw up the lists and plan your change of command. Children can help; they like to be included in planning, and they may be more enthusiastic about taking on some of the family responsibilities if they have a voice in making the lists of jobs for the family. When you have your ceremony, hand family members their lists and small flags after you've read the lists out loud. This signifies that they accept the responsibilities delegated to them. You may even want to have a cake and punch reception after your ceremony to make the atmosphere similar to a real change of command celebration.

Your family may choose to make a family duty roster that resembles a military roster. A two-column chart might list in one column what each family member's jobs are now, and parallel on another column list the jobs each will have while Dad is gone. Dad's job could be listed as his military mission or as the long distance communicator—be creative. You may want to add a slogan, such as "All valued members of the family team working together," to your chart. The chart could be hung on the refrigerator or somewhere the children will see it every day.

Each deployment is different, and changes occur from one year to another, so even if you've prepared for previous family separations it's necessary to prepare yourselves for the one coming next. Your plan probably needs to be revised and updated. Military families need to "Be flexible in everything. Military life has no room for rigidity. . . . Military service isn't a job. It's a lifestyle."[5] The lifestyle affects the whole family, and preparing for each new experience will help them enjoy, and sometimes endure, the unique life of the military family.

PREPARING YOUR CHILDREN

Children resist change and don't always understand how to express their fears and feelings verbally. The first thing you can do to prepare them for separation is tell them what will happen. When you tell them about a deployment early, they will have time to think about it and adjust to the idea. If your children are old enough to understand it, tell them the purpose of your deployment. They need to know that you're leaving because you have to work in a different place for a while, and that you leaving home has nothing to do with anything they did.

Children always watch their parents and imitate aspects of their behavior. That's one way they learn. They will watch you respond to the impending separation too, and your response will show them how to act. If possible, involve them in your plans for the separation. You may want to go to the library to check out books that deal with family separations or changes, or look for information on the Internet together. For example, the story of Mr. Roundhead on www.tckworld.com, or the web sites operated by the National Institute for Building Long Distance Relationships.

If you do things with your children to help them understand what family separation is like, they may realize that they will be able to adjust to the changes. Books can help them understand that they don't have to be afraid when a parent goes away, and that the parent still loves them. You can also use books or the Internet to find information about where Dad is going. Children will enjoy learning what the place is like, what customs people there have, and what kinds of foods they eat.

Maybe before you deploy you could spend time with each child, doing what that child likes to do, and possibly have a picture taken of you during the activity. For small children, the activity may be going to the park to swing, or going to the zoo. For some, it may mean going to a pizza place and playing video games. Others may want to go bike riding, play catch or basketball, or go to a mall. Doing things together that the children like to do makes it easier for them to talk about what's on their minds, because the adult is entering into *their* world of interest. You may want to make a "date" with them to do the activity again as soon as you return.

Involve the Children in Your Planning

Children need reassurance of both parents' love for them; they need the security of knowing that love does not change when you are separated. Children need to know you'll be thinking about them while you're gone. They may enjoy preparing a Deployment Calendar so they can mark off the days while Dad is gone. (Scriptographic Booklets has a coloring calendar for military families, called *Deployment Days*. For ordering information, refer to "Resources to Help Children," following this section, below.) If children have a way to measure how long Dad will be gone, they may be able to accept his absence better because they are reminded that it will end.

They may enjoy writing letters to Dad while he is gone and look forward to receiving mail from him. Dad may want to buy cards, postcards, and stamps to take along, so he can send personal greetings to each child and to his wife. The Write Connection company publishes letter-writing kits they call WriteBack Mail that are designed to facilitate adult and child pen pal relationships. Channing-Bete offers a "Write From the Heart" kit for children. (If your family wants to know more about these kits, refer to "Resources to Help Children," following this section, below.)

Dad may want to write small messages to each child, which can be put into capsules and given to the children like a daily or weekly vitamin pill from Dad. Children may want to help by addressing envelopes for Dad to take along and putting stamps on them. Dad may want to buy some gift certificates to his children's favorite restaurants, such as McDonald's, to take along to mail to the children during the deployment.

Before leaving, Dad or Mom could lie down on a piece of paper, and let the family draw his or her outline. Then each day he or she is away, the children could add a decoration to the outline by coloring, with markers, or stickers. The children could lie down on the outline and pretend they're getting their daily hug from Dad or Mom.

Maybe your family would enjoy making t-shirts with each family member's handprint on them, to wear for family solidarity during the deployment. Knowing Dad or Mom has his or her shirt along on the deployment may make this a child's favorite shirt to wear.

Some families find that if Dad makes each child a chart to record their daily chores, behavior, or activities, the children feel connected to him through the use of the chart. If Dad is on a Navy cruise, a cruise map could be made so the family can mark his progress during the separation. Including pictures of Dad at work, using colorful stickers, and following Dad's travel route with a marker can make the project more fun. The children learn geography in the process, and might even want to take the chart to school for show and tell![6] If Dad is not on a ship, your family can still use the cruise map idea, revising the map to fit your circumstances.

Maybe your map will have airplanes or tanks on it to mark where Dad is located.

Any map or chart that Dad prepares for use during the separation will help children feel closer to him after he's gone. As they use the visual aid, they will remember the preparation of it and that Dad cares so much about them that he wanted to do something special for them before he left. You can find more ideas to help you stay close to your children in *The Business Traveling Parent,* by Dan Verdick. This book is available in most bookstores; if the bookstore nearest you doesn't have it, they can order it for you.

Before Dad leaves, both parents and children should have a clear understanding of family rules and methods of discipline. Then, when he is gone, family patterns can continue smoothly. There are some excellent books available to help parents decide how to build their family rules and communicate them to their children. Two of the best are *Dare to Discipline,* by Dr. James Dobson, and *Withhold Not Correction,* by Bruce Ray. They are both available in libraries or can be purchased in bookstores. These books stress what separated families soon discover: developing and maintaining a predictable pattern of routine and discipline helps children feel secure. The "For Parents Only" series booklets published by the Bureau For At-Risk Youth also address specific aspects of nurturing children. (Refer to "Resources to Help Children," following this section, below, for information about how to find all of these great publications.)

Children appreciate being included in preparing for Dad's departure. Maybe your children could help you pack (roll up your socks, fold towels or handkerchiefs, etc.). Ask each child if he or she has something they'd like to give you to take along to remind you of them while you're gone. Just be sure it isn't valuable or too large to fit into the duffle bag, so it isn't cumbersome. Maybe they have a favorite picture you could take, a small plastic toy, a favorite washcloth or towel for you to use, some stickers, or a few of their favorite decorative Band-Aids for blisters.

Try to give each child something of yours to help them remember that you think of them individually while you are gone. You might want to give them your baseball cap, an old military hat, a uniform patch or pin, a key ring, a handkerchief with your initial on it, or anything else that represents a special connection between you and that child.

Spouses naturally think of equipping each other with a phone list before they deploy, and may even tell them how to get in touch with someone in the unit, but what about the children? Can we assume correctly that since a parent is there with the children, they'll have all the support they need? Don't forget that a parent is also missing, and the child feels that void. The parent who is at home may not be able to fill that void alone. If a single parent is deployed, the void is intensified for children. Before you deploy, help your children understand that after they leave there are people they can talk to or do activities with, and be sure they feel comfortable approaching those people and know how to contact them.

Sensitivity to Children's Emotional Responses

Children don't like change, but they can sense when something like a family separation is about to happen and will respond better if they are included in the preparation in at least a small way. Find time to get your family together to talk about it. Older children might be able to tell younger brothers and sisters what a previous deployment was like.

Explain at each child's level why you are leaving, where you are going (generally, if not specifically; depending on the security of your orders, you may have to say only that you are going overseas, or you may be free to tell them exactly where you'll be), who you are going with (maybe they have a friend whose Dad will be deploying with you), and how long you expect to be gone (you may not know, in which case you should tell them that you don't know, but you hope to be home before some date or celebration they can relate to and that they look forward to every year). Always use your most *pessimistic* estimate of the amount of time you'll be away—it's better for children to be surprised at an early return than disappointed that you didn't return when you said you would.

Children may think their father is leaving because of something they did, or that they are being abandoned by him. Taking time to prepare children for family separations helps them understand that they aren't being deserted and that they aren't responsible for Dad's absence. Whatever their level of understanding, try to help them relate your absence to your work.[7] It helps children to visualize what that means if you've taken them to a family day or have pictures of your workplace.

It can help your children if you voice your own ambivalent feelings about being separated. Then your children know that you have feelings like theirs, and they can see you model appropriate ways to release feelings by talking about them.[8] As they talk about their feelings, be a sensitive listener. You don't have to answer all of their questions; it's all right to admit you don't have all of the answers. They need you to be honest with them and sensitive to their reactions to change.

When we got orders to go to Okinawa, our oldest son, Mike, who was in Junior High at the time, said he wasn't going, so we didn't need to get him a plane ticket. We asked him why, and he said he didn't want to live outside of America, especially so far away where people didn't speak English. After few weeks went by, we told Mike we'd be picking him and Dan up from school a little early the next day so we could get our passports. He said he didn't need one, because he wasn't going. We asked him whether he thought he might like to come and visit us sometime while we lived over there, and after he thought about it for a moment, he said, "Well, I guess so."

"Then you'll need a passport, Mike."

"OK, but I'm not going to Okinawa, so don't get me a plane ticket! I'll only get the passport for a visit."

By the time we had to get the plane tickets and board the plane, Mike was ready to go. I think he knew all along that he wouldn't have a choice, and would be moving with us. But, he needed time to express and process what he was feeling without being told he shouldn't feel like he did, or being judged or disciplined for his response. Give your children time to process their emotions, like Mike needed before we went to Okinawa.

Open communication helps your children understand that they're important to you. So does spending time with them. Before you leave on your deployment, make it a priority to spend time with each child doing the things he or she enjoys doing with you most, whether that is playing a game, going for a walk, going out for ice cream, or going fishing. If someone can take pictures of the two of you during the activity, the picture will be a special memory for the child to hold on to while you're gone.

If you feel like you need help preparing your children for a family separation, there are organizations that can give you advice or provide activities to help your children. Among them are the Family Service or Support Center, chapel or church, recreation center, youth center, child development center, school, library, civilian boys or girls clubs, Red Cross, YMCA, mental health clinics, and counseling centers.

1. USAF Chaplain Service Institute. *Link: Staying Together While Apart.* Maxwell AFB, AL: USAF Chaplain Service Institute, June 1994: 4.
2. Roberts, Sue. "Separated!" in *Deployed, Not Disconnected: Hope and Help For Husbands and Wives Facing Separations Due to Military Assignments,* ed. Don and Karen Martin. (Englewood, CO: Officer's Christian Fellowship Books, 1991), 47.
3. DOD Office of Family Policy, Support & Services. *1992 DOD Surveys of Officers and Enlisted Personnel and Their Spouses: Individual and Family Readiness for Separation and Deployment.* Rockville, MD: Westat, Inc.: 5-7.
4. Graham, Lieutenant Colonel Ward, U. S. Air Force (Retired). "Fulfilling a Husband's Responsibility," in *Deployed, Not Disconnected: Hope and Help for Husbands and Wives Facing Separations Due to Military Assignments,* ed. Don and Karen Martin. (Englewood, CO: OCF Books, 1991), 30.
5. Cline, 242.
6. McColl, Denise. *Footsteps of the Faithful.* (Moscow, ID: Community Christian Ministries, Inc., 1995), 112.
7. See page 11 of *Daddy's Days Away,* produced by the Family Programs Branch Headquarters, U. S. Marine Corps, for ideas about how to do this.
8. Navy Family Services Center. *Navy Family Deployment Guide.* Norfolk, VA, 1987: 49.

· 5 ·

FAMILY DEPLOYMENT GUIDE

Families may want to develop checklists of things to do to prepare for military separations. This is important for Reserve and Guard families, as well as those on Active Duty. Checklists should be reviewed every year to be sure they are still effective. If you put all of your ideas into a notebook or an accordion file, it will be easier to organize the information into a usable format. Practically, where do you start to do this? You may want to divide your information into topical sections. Here are some ideas you may want to include as you consider making a Deployment Guide for your family.

FINANCES

One of the most important places to begin can be the family budget and financial practices. The financial circumstances of military families can change frequently because of their mobile lives, and their financial plans should be flexible. Budgets must be continually revised and updated to remain useful. How sensitive to change is your financial plan? Who takes care of the bills? Does the other spouse know how to do it, too? If the husband is deployed on short notice, there may not be time to show the wife how to pay bills before he leaves. Husband and wife should be equally qualified and knowledgeable about how to run the household finances. Specifically, they should each know the following:

Bank Accounts

- Account number, type of account, bank's name, address, and telephone number for each bank account (checking and saving); do you both know how to use Automatic Teller Machine (ATM) cards?
- Do you have a safe deposit box? Where? Do you know how to get into it?
- What investments do you have? List the agents, companies, and account numbers for investments, including stocks and bonds. Remember to include the Thrift Savings Plan (TSP) information for federal employees, if you participate in that plan through payroll deduction. What percentage of your pay is deducted into your TSP account, and how is it invested? Be sure your spouse knows where this information is located.
- What loans do you have? When and where do you make payments? What is the minimum payment that can be made? Will deployment affect the amount of payment or rate of interest? You may want to ask your lender those questions.
- Do you know how to balance the checkbook to the monthly statement and maintain the checking account? Who do you call at the bank if there is a problem balancing the account? Be sure to keep track of your checking account balance. Bounced checks cost you money and damage your credit, and knowingly writing a check with insufficient funds is a violation of the Uniform Code of Military Justice and will result in harsh penalties.
- Is the checking account in both the husband's and wife's names? It is better if the account is registered in *both* names and set up so that if one party should die the account is automatically the property of the other. In some cases, an account registered in two names must go to probate in case of death. You may want to ask your bank about your account to be sure your money

would be immediately available to the spouse if one of you died.

- How does your pay get into your account? Do you have direct deposit? If you don't have direct deposit, visit your military finance office immediately to get it started. You are allowed allotments to other accounts if you don't want all of the pay to go into a single checking account.
- How do you order new checks when they are needed? How many do you order, and is it important that you keep the same type of checks?
- Where do you keep the monthly leave and earnings statement (LES)? Is it mailed to your home or work address? If you are deployed, will your spouse still regularly receive the LES?

Each military family should have a plan, ready to activate on a moment's notice, for handling the finances in case of a sudden deployment. You may not have enough notification to get a plan together before a spouse leaves.

However, deployment isn't the only reason to have a plan for handling finances from separate locations. Many military members frequently go on temporary duty away from their families. Along with deployments, temporary absences may increase due to recent changes in the military.

You may want to have a separate account to use as the temporary duty or deployment account to keep your household financial plan flexible and efficient. Open the account in the names of both spouses, so both will have access to it. You may want to keep only the minimum balance in the account when he is not away from home, but try to keep a balance in the account that will give your husband enough money for at least the first month he is gone. You can decide what that amount should be for your family. If both names are on the account, the husband can take the checkbook along when he is deployed, and the wife will be able to make deposits as necessary (keep deposit slips on hand, so they aren't all deployed with your husband), depending on the length of the separation. Your family might prefer to have a regular allotment going into the account. Set up the allotment now; it often takes a few months to get an allotment working smoothly.

Many military members have government credit cards that *must* be used for official travel and expenses. Remember that the government credit cards *must* be paid in full when the bill comes each month, and that they are not for personal use. If you decide to open a TDY/deployment checking account, you may want to use that account to pay the government credit card bill when it comes. If the military member is gone for an extended period of time, the bill may arrive before the deployment or TDY is complete, but the bill must still be paid.

Talk to your military finance office about how to keep your account current. You may be eligible for an advance in pay to cover the bill, or an automatic payment to the credit card account. Your spouse can write a check to pay the bill, but cannot conduct any other business related to the card, including talking to finance about how to keep payment current, or even changing your address. The regulations regarding use of these credit cards are strict, and you don't want misuse or late payments to mar your credit rating *or* your military career.

Housing

- Do you own a home? When and where do you make payments? Are taxes and insurance paid separately or included in your monthly payment? If separately, when are they due?
- If you are renting, who is your landlord and when is your rent due? Keep the landlord's address and phone number available. Did you sign a lease for a specific amount of time? Will it expire while you are deployed? If so, does your wife need a Power of Attorney to renew it?
- Are you on a waiting list for military housing? What will your family do if they are offered housing while you are gone? Can they accept it and move in? If they accept government housing in your absence, they will need Powers of Attorney to accept the house and arrange the move. If they are offered housing and turn it down, will you still be eligible to receive quarters

later? How would a turndown affect your place on the waiting list?

- What is the process for moving your household goods? If it became necessary to move without you, does your wife know how to handle it?
- Where are the rental or lease agreements, deed to your home, real estate records, and appraisals or mortgage information?

Bill Paying

- Do you know what bills to expect on a monthly basis and how to pay them (by mail, at the bank, at the place of business, etc.)?
- Who owes you money? Whom do you owe? When and how are payments made?
- Do you have any purchases on layaway or DPP? How do you keep them current?
- Make a record of credit card numbers and their issuers' phone numbers and addresses (and similar information for anything else in your wallet, such as ATM cards and PIN numbers for accounts); include instructions for reporting lost cards.
- When do annual, semiannual, or quarterly payments or bills come due and how are they budgeted to be paid?
- Do you know how and where to file federal, state, and city income tax forms? Who prepares your tax forms? Remember to allow time to mail the tax return back and forth for both spouses' signatures, and always make copies in case forms are lost in the mail.
- Do you have a cell phone that you won't need during the deployment? Will you cancel that service? Who do you call to activate or deactivate your cell phone service?
- Do you live in an area where you use ration cards or gas coupons? Will they expire during the separation? How are they renewed, obtained, and used?
- What insurance policies do you have? List insurance policies for coverage of life, automobile, home, household goods, property, long-term care, and medical, along with the policy

numbers and expiration dates of each policy. Include the in-surance agents' names, phone numbers, and addresses.

• Do you have a budget to help you spend your income wisely? Monthly expenses you may want to consider including in your budget are: housing, home repairs, utilities (gas, oil, electric, coal, water), telephone (local and long distance carriers, and cell phone, if you have one), food (including school lunches, eating out, groceries, meat, pet food, holiday treats), babysitters, clothing, dry cleaning, debts (payments, loans, car, credit cards, layaway, DPP purchases), club memberships, car upkeep and gas, insurance (car, household goods, life, health, long-term care), school (books, fees, tuition, general supplies), children's allowance, music lessons or instruments, recreation (entertain-ment, travel, parties, sports activities or teams that children are involved in), cable TV, Internet charges, savings, invest-ments, holiday gifts and spending, emergencies, gifts, etc. Hav-ing at least a guide for your budget will help ensure that you plan properly for your expenses. Added expenses during de-ployment might include extra uniforms, food, telephone calls, postage and stationery, toiletries, and entertainment and per-sonal expenses for your husband. Are you prepared for those extra expenses or planning how you will meet them? If you need help planning your budget, your Family Support or Ser-vice Center may be able to help you make a realistic plan.

When both spouses are equipped to handle ongoing financial matters in the home, they may want try to develop a system in which they take turns paying the bills so they are both comfort-able with their ability to handle the process. They should both be familiar with the family checking account and the account you may use for temporary duty or deployments. As you consider the balance you will keep in your deployment or temporary duty ac-count, remember that your budget may be tighter while you're separated.

Even if your husband is deployed in tent conditions and field rations, he will want and need money for things like writing materials, postage, and personal hygiene items, and your family's needs at home will also go on. Expect the deployment to strain your budget and add to your costs. If you plan for a tighter budget before it is necessary, you and your family will be able to deal with it better if it costs you more to live apart than it does for you to live together.

If the financial strain of a deployment becomes great enough that you fall behind on a scheduled payment, write a letter to the company explaining your situation, and try to make at least a partial payment. Although you'll have to pay more interest and service charges, the company will likely extend the payment period because you are making an effort to pay what you owe them. Your installation has financial counselors to help you plan your budget and teach you how to manage when the strain becomes too much. Call your Family Support Center or Family Service Center for help.

You may decide to keep your entire household budget and financial matters separate from your *Family Deployment Guide*, but be sure both spouses agree to and understand your plan. Then learning how to do everything and finding out where everything is will not be part of the goodbye process.

IMPORTANT PAPERS

Each family has important papers that need to be organized and accessible to the wife during a military separation. It may be most helpful to keep them in a safe place and list them in your *Family Deployment Guide*, along with the location of each document. You may want to put a copy of each document in your *Deployment Guide*, including instructions to find the original. If you don't have everything on the following list, you may want to begin to accumulate them if they apply to your family situation. Know where these documents are and keep them available.

Legal Records

- Power of Attorney: There are general and specific POAs. A general POA allows the person you designate to have unlimited authority to sign your name or act on your behalf. It should be used cautiously because it allows another person to do any legal act in your name. A special POA is more limited, and gives the person you designate power to do only what you specifically request him or her to do. You might use a special POA to enable someone to cash your checks, secure a loan, ship your household goods, sign damage claims, accept quarters, sign agreements for home rental or purchase, give your consent for someone to obtain medical care for your children, or other specific acts you may need accomplished. The special POA should be used whenever it meets your needs. POAs are valid only while the person granting the POA is alive. A POA cannot be used to start, stop, or change your military pay allotments. Because some organizations hesitate to accept a POA, make your POA as specific as you can to increase the possibility that it will be honored. Remember that POAs expire and must be updated yearly. Your legal office can help you determine what exact POAs you may need.
- List names and phone numbers of your personal lawyer or any trusted friends who may be consulted about your personal or business affairs in your absence.
- Will: Both spouses should have a will. The wills should be reviewed and updated periodically. Situations that require updating your will include: a substantial change in the value of your assets (such as receiving an inheritance), birth or death of an immediate family member, change in your state of legal residence, your executor dies or is no longer competent, a guardian must be appointed for your children, a change in marital status, certain provisions need to be changed, or there are changes in property ownership. You may also want to consider having a living will. A living will informs a hospital of your wishes regarding your medical treatment if you become incapacitated. To be sure your will is honored according to your

wishes, find out if your state of residence or home of record has any special requirements.

- What burial instructions do you have? Do you own a cemetery plot?
- Marriage License, Divorce Decrees, Court Orders relating to children, prenuptial agreements.
- Death Certificates.
- Birth Certificates, baptismal certificates, adoption papers.
- Citizenship papers, naturalization papers.
- Social Security cards and numbers for each family member. Keep a separate list of each person's Social Security Number (SSN).
- Discharge papers (DD 214).
- Passports: In addition to the passports, keep a list of each person's passport number, where it was issued, the date it was issued, and the date it expires. You need that information to replace or renew passports.
- Copies of your current military PCS orders and your deployment orders. Include Privately-Owned Vehicle (POV) shipping documents, if applicable.

Health Records
- Health and immunization records for family pets.
- Immunization records for each family member, health records for any family member with special requirements (including chronic health problems, allergies, etc.), as well as location of each family member's medical records. Are immunization records up to date?
- Copies of eyeglass prescriptions, and records of medications taken regularly by anyone in the family.
- Do you know how to use the military medical and dental facilities? Keep central appointments, emergency, and other applicable phone numbers where you can find them easily.
- When do your family members need their next dental or orthodontic visit? What provider do you go to? If you do not receive care in a military facility, how is payment made? Do you have insurance to help cover the cost?

- Do you know how to get medical care when you need it? Do you know procedures for using military medical treatment facilities and for using TRICARE? If you know how to use these benefits and have the paperwork available, then when a need arises and your sponsor is gone you will not have trouble getting the care you need.
- Do you have medical insurance, including secondary policies such as Civilian Health and Medical Program of the Uniformed Services (CHAMPUS) or TRICARE supplemental policies? Do you know how to file claims and where to mail them?

Personal Records

- Keep a record of military identification (ID) card numbers of each family member, and dates of expiration. Do they need to be renewed soon? If they expire in the sponsor's absence, do you know how to get them renewed?
- Are your dependents all enrolled in Defense Enrollment Eligibility Reporting System (DEERS)?
- Copies of temporary or PCS orders.
- Resume of each spouse and transcripts (or address of school(s) to which the request for transcripts would be sent), if applicable. Are you or your spouse taking any classes? Will you try to continue, or have to drop them? Talk to your school representative as soon as you are notified of your deployment.
- School record of each child, listing names, addresses, and phone numbers of each school each child has attended, and report cards.
- Income tax records.
- Official military records or documents, including copies of requests for allotments and information about your TSP account, if you have one.
- Automobile or motorcycle title and registration for each vehicle. Do you have a boat or other type of recreational vehicle that you need a title or registration for?
- Do you have extra keys for your car, house, or safe deposit box? Where are they kept?

HOUSEHOLD MANAGEMENT

As you continue to prepare your *Family Deployment Guide*, include a separate page or section for household items that may need attention or maintenance during the separation. The following items are things you'll want to consider as you do this:

Automobile Care

- Automobile (list separately for each car): What kind of gas does your car use? Does your family know how to check the oil and tires? How much air goes in the tires? Can each driver change a flat tire? When does the oil need to be changed? How much and what kind of oil does it need? What about filters? How often does the car need to be tuned up? Do you have a maintenance schedule for the family to follow? What kind of battery does the car need if they have to replace it? What size and type of tires do you use? How can you tell if they need to be replaced? Where should they be bought? What kind of muffler does your car have? If it needs to be replaced, where should it be purchased? Where should the car be taken for repair if there is a breakdown (list the name, phone number, and address)? When does the vehicle registration tag (military installation sticker) and inspection or safety sticker (where required) expire? How can it be renewed? When do your license plates need to be renewed? Does your family know how to do that, where to go to do it, and what paperwork or fees they'll need to take along? Who is your automobile insurance agent (list the agent's name, phone number, address, and your policy number)? Does each driver know what to do in case of an accident? Where, how much, and when do the insurance payments need to be paid? Is the car paid for? If so, where is the title? If not, who holds the lien? When, how much, and where are loan payments made?
- Are you living in an area where you use gas coupons, or do you pay for gas with cash or a credit card? How and where do you get gas coupons? What paperwork is needed? What kind of gas does your car use?

- Do you belong to an auto club? Do you have towing service? What are the phone numbers for these services? When are dues payable, how much, and where are payments made?
- Do you have a first aid kit, flashlight, maps, and extra water or other weather-appropriate supplies in your car?

Home Maintenance

- Lawn Care: Does the family know how to operate and maintain the lawn mower? Do they know what kind of oil and fuel it uses? If they aren't sure, take them outside for a lesson or make a plan together for how the yard will be cared for. If the lawn mower breaks down, where do they take it for repair?
- Furnace/Air-Conditioning Maintenance: Does your family know how to check and change the air filters? What type and size filters are required? Do you have extras available? Where do you go to buy them? How often do you change them? Does the unit need servicing periodically? How often and when? How is your system fueled? Do you need heating oil or coal? Where do you get fuel? Who does the servicing and maintenance? (List the service company name, address, and phone number.)
- Household Inventory: Do you have a list of your household items, appliances, and electronic equipment and their serial numbers? Most insurance companies recommend that you take pictures of electronic equipment and appliances that have serial numbers and keep the pictures with those serial numbers. You also need this information for military moves. Some items you may want to check for serial numbers are: refrigerators, ovens, portable dishwashers, TVs, VCRs, CD or DVD players, other stereo component parts, all computer components, sewing machines, bicycles, treadmills or other sports equipment, lawn mowers, and humidifiers.
- Do you have a list of repair services to call if anything in the house breaks down? (Plumber, heating/furnace maintenance and repair, air conditioning, electrician, washer and dryer, water heater, dishwasher, garbage disposal, oven, microwave, refrigerator, computer, stereo equipment, bicycles, etc.)

- Does the family know the location of the fuse box or electric control panel for your house or apartment? Do they know how to operate the breaker switches and change fuses? Do you have extra fuses?
- Bicycles: Do the family bicycles need to be registered or licensed? If so, when do they expire and how will they be renewed?
- Home Security: Do all of your windows have locks that work? Does your family know how to test the smoke alarms and turn them off if they go off accidentally? Is each family member careful to keep the home secure—do they lock the house if no one is at home and during the night?
- Do you live in a climate that makes use of screens or storm windows as seasons change? Do you know how to change them and where they are stored? If they need repair, who do you call?
- Do you know how to check your roof for leaks and keep rain gutters cleared of leaves? Who do you call for roof repairs?
- Do you have a fireplace? Do you burn wood, or is it gas? Where do you get and store your firewood? Does your family know how to use the fireplace and ventilate the smoke correctly? Who do they call if they need to have the chimney cleaned? It should be checked every year if you use the fireplace regularly. Does everyone in the family know how to clean the hearth and safely dispose of remnants from the fireplace?
- Do you have a pool or spa? Is your family safety-conscious about its use? Do they know how to care for it and treat it with chemicals? Where do you buy the chemicals? Does it matter what brand you use? Who is responsible for the regular maintenance? Does it need to be drained or treated for seasonal changes throughout the year? Who do you call for service or problems?
- Where are your family's tools? Does everyone know how to use tools (flashlight, hammer, nails, masking tape, wrench, regular and Phillips screwdrivers, pliers, etc.) for basic repairs?
- Where does your family keep extra light bulbs and batteries?

Family Management

- Key phone number list: you may want to keep a list of telephone numbers for key military installation facilities near your telephone. Many military Family Support Centers provide a magnetized list of all base and civilian key telephone numbers for families to put on their refrigerators. The numbers listed may include hospital emergency room, poison control, Security Forces/Military Police, fire, base operator, chaplain, chaplain non-duty hours, Red Cross, Family Support Center/Army Community Service, First Sergeant, Commander, hospital central appointments, vet clinic, and household maintenance. You may want to include names and numbers of neighbors, friends, or relatives.

- Emergency Numbers: Do you have a list of all phone numbers that might be needed to take care of an emergency near your phone? Remember that if a babysitter takes your children to a hospital he or she must have a Power of Attorney along with proper ID in order to receive care. Have you provided for that possibility?

- Household Chores: Do both parents know what must be done to keep the house clean and orderly? Do both parents know what chores are suitable for each child by age, and which chores the children do regularly? Do you have a schedule for routine chores? If the person who likes to do the cooking is deployed, what plan will your family follow for meals? Who will cook and do the grocery shopping?

- Laundry: Do you know how to sort and wash the clothes? What laundry products do you use? Do you know what things have to be machine or hand washed? Hot or cold water? Do all of your clothes dry in the dryer? At what settings? If they don't go in the dryer, what care do you give them? What has to be ironed? How hot should the iron be? Do you use steam? What water do you use for the iron? Read labels on clothing for help.

- Hygiene: Do you normally wash your children's hair, bathe them, or supervise their teeth care? Are they brushing every day? If a child is too young to fix her own hair, do both parents know how to do it?

- Clothing: Do both parents know what stores to shop at for clothes for each of the children? Do both know what amount of clothing each child needs at one time, and any special requirements (ballet, soccer, band, etc.)?

· 6 ·

Preparation for Single Parent and Dual-Military Families

If you are a single parent or dual-military family, you have additional requirements. Do your relatives know how to contact you if there is an emergency? Does your unit know how to contact your relatives and your children's caregiver? Do you have someone to take care of your car and your mail while you are deployed? What about finances? Perhaps you have only your own name on your checking account. Who will pay your bills for you while you're gone? Car payments, insurance, credit card statements, etc., will continue. Should you add someone's name to your checking account or get someone a power of attorney to take care of your bills? How will you file your tax returns while you're gone? If something happens to you, does your will specifically designate what your wishes are for your finances? Even more important than that, however, is the care of your children.

The military requires you to designate someone to care for your children if you are deployed or separated from your family. Your family care plan may need to be revised every time you move to a new duty assignment. When the Defense Advisory Committee on Women in the Services (DACOWITS) went to visit military installations in Europe, they found that the concern of childcare was straining military members. "Troops told committee members that they had prepared family care plans that were not complete or reliable," and, "The report said many commanders acknowledged they had not consistently evaluated the plans submitted by their troops."[1] If the plan you make won't work, your family will suffer when you're deployed. Make sure your plan is workable—without depending on your commander to tell you what parts of your plan need improvement.

Your plan should provide for both short-term and long-term care of your children in your absence. You should have an alternate caregiver selected in case your caregiver becomes unable to take care of your children. Can you financially meet the demands of the plan you have made? If you can't afford to send your children to the person you choose as caregiver, your plan won't work. Remember to consider everything, including costs, as you make your decisions.

You've probably already filled out a Dependent Care Certificate, but if you haven't, do it now. Do you need to make temporary arrangements for someone to care for your children until your designated caregiver arrives, or until your children can be sent to the caregiver? Will your children be cared for in your home? Your *Family Deployment Guide* should include the following information for the person who cares for your children in your absence:[2]

- Names, phone numbers, and addresses of your extended family members.
- Name of your duty station or ship and duty mailing address.
- Does your unit know where your children will be? Give your unit the name, address, and phone number of your caregiver.
- Name and phone number of your commanding officer and First Sergeant (and Ombudsman, if applicable).
- Detailed information about each child, including full name, birth date, birthplace, favorite toys and foods, special comforts (pacifier or blanket), fears, and habits.
- For school-aged children: name of teachers, grade, school, and phone numbers. (Remember to update this every year.)

- Religious preference and place of worship. What are your desires for church attendance and the children's religious instruction in your absence?
- Note where your child's medical records are kept, any medication your child may be on, along with instructions about why the child needs it, how much, and for how long it is to be taken. List your pediatrician's name and telephone number. Make sure your caregiver has a POA for your child's medical care.
- Make sure each child has a valid military dependent ID card. If the cards expire and you are absent, how will they be renewed? Your caregiver should also have access to copies of your children's birth certificates and a record or photocopy of their ID cards. If your children lost their ID cards while you were gone, how would they be replaced?
- Dentist's name, address, and phone number; frequency of visits, when next appointment is due to be scheduled (also for orthodontist, if applicable).
- Your expectations and standards for discipline. You might want to make a note of specific methods of discipline you use, or what works best for a particular child.
- Who to contact in case of an emergency. Be sure your caregiver knows how to get assistance through the Red Cross, Family Support or Family Services, Accounting and Finance, the Legal Office, Chaplains, and Personal Affairs.
- Names and phone numbers of friends who might be resources for the caregiver.
- Do you expect the caregiver to attend parent conferences at school? If not, who will? You may want to give your children's teachers some self-addressed and stamped envelopes and ask them to use them to keep you informed of your children's school progress.
- Ask your caregiver for a regular description of your children's growth and development. Knowing what they are doing at each stage of growth will help you feel included in their care.

- Make sure there is a clear understanding of who possesses legal custody of your children. If you have custody as a result of divorce, give the caregiver a copy of the divorce document. The caregiver also needs a POA to act in *loco parentis* (as parent).
- Do you need these documents: Special Power of Attorney, Custody Agreement, Hold Harmless Agreement (if caregiver lives in military housing)?
- How will you arrange your finances to enable your caregiver to support your dependents?
- Do you need to get your caregiver access to the military installation? Do you need to get your caregiver access to the commissary and exchange? Even if the caregiver is not eligible for these benefits, she can purchase items for your dependents' use.
- Is there a pre-deployment briefing you can ask your caregiver to attend with you? Is your caregiver interested in being included in any family support groups that may be available while you're gone?
- What documents do you have to get notarized?
- Be sure your will has guardianship provisions.
- Review all of the above every year to be sure it is still in effect.

HOW TO GET THE FORMS AND DOCUMENTS YOU NEED

- Dependent Care Certification: See your unit orderly room. If you have questions, ask the orderly room clerk, First Sergeant, or Commander.
- Birth Certificate Copies: Request copies from the state of birth. You can call your military personnel customer service for each state's vital statistics office.
- Social Security Number: Ask your military personnel customer service for information.
- Special ID cards for children under age ten: Ask your military personnel customer service for information. The most

common reason a child under age ten would need an ID card is that the dependent is leaving the area to live with a caregiver during the sponsor's absence. In that case, the ID would be necessary to use CHAMPUS or TRICARE. This type of ID is limited to the time you are absent, and you need orders to process the card.

- Paperwork to make the caregiver a Commissary Agent: Obtain a Commissary Agent Letter from your military personnel customer services. The letter can be drafted close to the time you leave. It requires the name and address of the caregiver of your dependent and the dates the caregiver will need commissary access. Proof of dependency and inclusive dates of the sponsor's absence are also required. The caregiver, as your agent, is permitted to purchase items at the Exchange and the Commissary only for the dependent, not for themselves. You may want to ask whether unexpected delays in your return will affect your caregiver's access after your projected return date.

- Paperwork to give caregiver access to the installation: Your caregiver should be allowed on the military installation with a POA for that purpose. File a copy of the POA requesting installation access with the Security Forces (SF) or Military Police (MP), and your caregiver should always carry a copy. If the caregiver drives his or her own vehicle on the installation, it will have to be registered with Pass and ID.

- Powers of Attorney: Any POAs that you need may be obtained at your military legal office. You may need several specific POAs, and it is better to request several specific documents than one sweeping general POA.

- Paperwork to establish an allotment for the care of your dependents: Obtain paperwork from your military accounting and finance office. Make sure the allotment goes where you want it to (possibly a new account, opened for that purpose), and that your caregiver's name is also on the account (you can also make your dependent secondary to the caregiver).

Start all of the paperwork early or have it in place before you are notified of your next deployment so you don't have to rush to try to get it all done at the last minute. Ask your military legal office which documents need to be notarized.

Whether you entrust your children to a caregiver or the parent who is not deploying, you must be sure the appropriate person knows how to get medical care as it is needed. Because you are military, your dependents should have access to the nearest military medical facility. If care is not available there, or if you are too far away from a military facility to use one, do your dependents know how to use CHAMPUS and the TRICARE Health Care System? Ask your Health Benefits Advisor if you need more information.

1. Seabolt, Amee. "Child care, deployments worry service members, panel finds." *The Stars and Stripes*. 27 October 1996, p. 4.
2. The list includes ideas taken from: *Navy Family Deployment Guide*. Norfolk, VA: Navy Family Services Center, 1987: 53–56.

· 7 ·

MOBILIZATION OF NATIONAL GUARDS AND RESERVES

The Guards and Reserves are called to Active Duty more often now than they were in the past. They're no longer seen as weekend warriors, but as vital elements of the total military force. When Guard or Reserve members go to do their periodic duty, their families may not know much about what they do while serving. If at all possible, take your family to your Reserve or Guard center and show them what you do there.

Your unit may offer opportunities to introduce families to what Reserve or Guard members do on their duty days or when they mobilize or deploy. The Maryland Air National Guard's 175th Wing held a Family Deployment Day. Guard members showed their families the airplanes and work centers around the wing, and took them to visit booths explaining the role of legal, pay, insurance, and family readiness.

The 176th Wing at Kulis Air National Guard Base, in Anchorage, Alaska, held a weekend readiness conference to introduce family members to their mission and teach them how to prepare for deployments. While the military members performed their drill weekend, family members saw the aircraft, had lunch in the chow hall, and learned about the military structure and benefits. Their briefings included presentations about the commissary, the First

Sergeant's role, OPSEC (Operations Security), COMSEC (Communications Security), military pay, family programs, legal, and other military benefits and services, in addition to presentations that addressed preparing for deployments, getting through family separations, and reunion.

If your unit doesn't have an event to help family members understand your role in the military and its mission, you may want to suggest beginning one.

The more you can communicate to your family about what you do in the Reserves or Guards and make them familiar with the military system, the better equipped they will be to deal with the call to Active Duty and family separation. Try to visit with the families of others with whom you serve. Tell your family that it's likely that you will be called to Active Duty for a period of time, possibly without a lot of notice. Tell them what benefits they'll be eligible for if you're activated. If you aren't sure what those benefits are, ask the Family Service Center, someone in your chain of command, or your unit chaplain. Many families of Reservists haven't taken advantage of the support systems or benefits the military provides because they didn't know about them. Don't let that happen to your family.

As you consider how to care for your family as you prepare for mobilization or deployment, remember to fill out a Dependent Care Certification/Family Care Certification form. This form relates your temporary and permanent care arrangements for your family in your absence. If you are a single parent, you must have someone designated as a legal guardian in case you are activated. Lack of preparation for your family will not prevent you from leaving, but will make your departure more difficult for your family members when you go.

If you live near an Active Duty installation, help prepare your family for the possibility that you may be activated by taking your family to the installation to see where things are located. Then if you are mobilized, going to the installation for benefits or help will not be as difficult for or overwhelming to them. Give them the name and phone number of someone at the installation that they can call for help if you are activated. The branch of service of the installation nearest your family does not make a difference—military benefits are the same for everyone and available to anyone with a valid ID card.

ID CARDS AND ACTIVE DUTY BENEFITS

In most cases, Reservists or Guard members will have enough notification of being called to Active Duty that they can bring their families to installations to get military dependent ID cards. If your husband is activated or mobilized, he should get your family ID cards before he leaves. If that isn't possible, be sure he gives you copies of his official orders so you are able to use your military entitlements. The family also needs copies of the sponsor's orders after they have ID cards. Along with the ID cards, the orders are the legal document that verifies the family's eligibility for benefits on the installation.

Guard and Reserve members must enroll each family member in the Defense Eligibility Enrollment Reporting System (DEERS). Enrollment in DEERS allows your family access to military installations, commissary and exchange facilities, medical care, and other benefits. Even if you live too far from an Active Duty installation to use some of your other benefits, your family must be enrolled in DEERS to use medical benefits and TRICARE in civilian communities.

There is a booklet, entitled *A Guide to Reserve Family Benefits*, to help family members understand their entitlements, some of which have been recently enhanced. It is available from the Family Support organizations and on the Reserve Affairs home page: http://raweb.osd.mil/publications/index.htm. During deployments, many units and installations have meetings for spouses or families to help them understand their benefits, to identify needs, and to provide support. Chaplains know what their installations offer to families.

FAMILY SUPPORT PROGRAMS

Families may not feel the need for military support groups unless they develop a military-related need that the civilian community can't meet, such as problems with CHAMPUS or TRICARE. It is important for families to have connections to the military so that military needs can be met, even if these families don't live near installations.

If you are a Reservist or Guard member and are called to Active Duty but don't live near an installation, there still may be a support network available to your family. Ask what family programs are available before you deploy. Even if he or she is also being called to Active Duty, the chaplain is likely to be one of the first to know about family programs, since he or she is there to serve the needs of the people. (Refer to the "Taking Care of Yourself" segment of the "Deployment" section in this handbook for more information about support groups.) Preparation for how Reserve and Guard families will meet their needs and find support is an integral part of getting ready for the possibility of mobilization.

Many commands have family days and programs like the ones in Maryland and Alaska that include family briefings as part of mobilization exercises. Family briefings teach families about the role of the Reserves and Guards, the benefits that are available, and how to use the benefits. Awareness of the needs of families is reflected in the Family Support Program Advisory Committee, which was established in 1993. The committee works to develop plans and provide advice and ideas to meet needs when Reserve service members are mobilized. The Family Readiness Work Group meets quarterly to address issues of Reserve families. They send information to Family Program Managers who, in turn, pass the information to Reserve family members. Every Reserve unit has someone who acts as a point of contact for this group, so find out who the representative is at your Reserve unit.

Family Program Coordinators provide assistance to Reserve and Guard families when service members deploy, and work to help Family Support Groups. National Guard families should ask for their state's Family Program Coordinator, or the local contact to that person. Army Reserve families can find help at their Family Support Group, Family Support Liaison Officer, or unit administrator. The Air Force Reserve has civilian employees who work at the Family Readiness Centers to meet family needs. They also have a Reservist on staff who is a trained Family Readiness Technician, and is available when the unit is on an active-duty base. Many Air Force Reserve centers even have videophones for families to use when members are deployed. Naval Reserve, Marine Corps Reserve, and Coast Guard Reserve centers all have ombudsmen to help with family needs. Many ombudsmen are married to Reservists, and have first-hand experience in family separation issues. Ombudsmen can be found at the training centers.

In 1998 the first Joint Service Readiness Center opened in Minneapolis. The Air Force Reserve is the host unit, but other Reserve components are also involved. More Joint Service Centers will probably be opening as the military components work together rather than independently. Because the Reserve emphasis on Family Support is still emerging, military members should be attentive to what is available for families in their command. There is a complete list of Army Reserve Family Coordinators and National Guard Family Program Coordinators in *What's Next?: A Guide to Family Readiness for the Army Reserve*. Ask for this publication at your unit or your Family Services Center.

BENEFITS/ENTITLEMENTS

When Reservists are on Active Duty, their benefits normally include the following: access to most military facilities, use of exchange and commissary, use of dining facilities, limited medical and dental care, and access to most military recreational and entertainment facilities.[1] There are also some death benefits available to Reservists who die in connection with their military service.

Many states offer Reservists and Guard members benefits because of their military service. They may include exempting military pay from taxes, special license plates, and other leave and educational benefits. Check with your command or state to see what benefits may be available in your area.

When Reserve or Guard members are mobilized, their families are eligible to use certain military facilities, such as the commissary (non-profit grocery store on the installation) and the Post Exchange (PX) or Base Exchange (BX) (non-profit department store on the military installation). You need a valid military ID Card to use these facilities. If you haven't used military facilities before and are unsure about how to use them, find someone who knows the system to take you to the installation, show you around, and review the rules for using the facilities with you. At first it may seem overwhelming if you haven't used military facilities before, especially because you may be upset because of the mobilization. But it's worth the effort to become familiar with the system and use your benefits.

Guard and Reserve families that understand the military entitlements they have and support the duty of service members find that families can adjust to mobilization or deployment better when they are prepared. One wife who knew and used her entitlements said she saved money shopping at the exchange and commissary and that "being in the Reserve has helped me become more self-sufficient . . . I've surprised myself by learning to take care of these crises on my own. I guess that's what they mean by family readiness."[2]

Depending on the amount of time your husband serves on Active Duty, you may be entitled to health or other benefits. To help you learn what they are, get a copy of *Ordered to Active Duty—What Now? A Guide for Reserve Component Families,* available from most Reserve or Guard Units. Call your local unit to request a copy of this helpful publication if you don't have one. You can find telephone numbers for local Reserve or Guard units in the federal section of your telephone book. Your family will also benefit from making your own *Family Deployment Guide,* as described earlier in this book. The drastic change that mobilization may create for your family will be minimized if you have plans made and resources available to turn to during the deployment.

If you are not familiar with the military system, find out what is available to you while your husband is activated. That can be discouraging if you don't know where to start. However, the military system is not that difficult to approach, and is ready to answer your questions and help you use your benefits. If you don't know where to start, call the unit chaplain or your husband's supervisor or commander. If you don't know them, your husband has not given you the preparation for Active Duty that you need, but you can still find the answers. Look in your local telephone book's federal section for the military branch that is nearest you and tell them your husband has been activated and you do not know what benefits you are entitled to or how to go about using them. Also ask whether there are spouse or family support meetings in your area. If they cannot help you, they will refer you to the right office. It will be well worth the effort.

CIVILIAN SUPPORT FOR FAMILIES

Reserve and Guard families may have support groups available to them that meet many of their needs, but may not understand the military issues they encounter. There may not be other military families available to identify with if the Guard or Reserve member deploys individually or his whole unit does not go together. In some cases the unit may deploy as a whole, but since Reserve and Guard members often commute some distance to maintain their military commitment, there may not be families of the unit in your area. The potential for insufficient support during family separations is one of the most critical issues that Reserve and Guard families face. However, many Reserve and Guard families have established support systems in their civilian communities. They may have relatives or close friends, churches, or community involvements that provide stability and care for them during military separations.

DISRUPTION IN CIVILIAN EMPLOYMENT

Another important issue Reserve and Guard members have to address is the disruption in their civilian employment. When they are activated, Reserve and Guard members may experience financial strain because their military pay is not on the same scale as their civilian pay. People who are self-employed may wonder whether they will be able to keep up with their expenses and whether their businesses will continue in their absence. The Soldiers' and Sailors' Civil Relief Act is designed to assist those with needs beyond their control (see the current year's *Reserve Forces Almanac* or *National Guard Almanac*, or ask your legal office for more information). Reserve and Guard members should see whether they have the option of carrying pay insurance to protect their families from a disparity between military and civilian incomes.

When Reserve and Guard members return from deployments, their employers may give them different jobs than the ones they had before they were mobilized. The pay may be the same but the positions may be less career-enhancing. There is a law to help employers and employees coordinate civilian work with Reserve and Guard responsibilities. The Uniformed Services Employment and Reemployment Rights Act (USERRA) was signed into law in October 1994. It outlines the rights and responsibilities of Reserve and Guard members and of their civilian employers. USERRA requires Reserve and Guard members to give advance notice of upcoming military duty in order to retain eligibility for reemployment afterward (unless that is not possible because of the military mission). The employer is expected to give the member time off for duty and return the employee to his previous position afterward. Some Reserve and Guard members and employers may not be aware of all of the revisions in USERRA, and may want to review them. They are outlined in the *Reserve Forces Almanac*.

As a Reservist or Guard Member, you may have to negotiate with your civilian employer because of your military duty. Plan to keep your employer informed of your military duty as far in advance as possible, both verbally and by written memo. Maintaining good communication with civilian employers should keep military duty from becoming a problem. Most civilian employers are supportive of Reserve and Guard member employees. If you have a problem with your civilian employer that you can't resolve, you may want to ask your Unit Commander for advice. If the Unit Commander isn't able to help, you can call the National Committee for Employer Support of the Guard and Reserve (NCESGR) at (800) 336-4590. If you prefer to write to the NCESGR, their address is: 1555 Wilson Blvd., Suite 200, Arlington, VA 22209-2405. NCESGR also has state chairmen in every state. (Their names and addresses are listed in the *Reserve Forces Almanac* and the *National Guard Almanac*. Information about how to obtain these books is found in the Reserve and Guard Resources section in the back of this book.)

Although Reserve and Guard members and their families have some concerns that are different than those of Active Duty military, the needs of all military component families are similar. Reserve and Guard members are part of the Total Force, and are important to the military mission. Reserve and Guard families benefit from seeing themselves as military families, whether in part-time or full-time service.

1. Hunter, Ronald S., MSG Gary L. Smith, USA (Retired), and Debra M. Gordon, editors. *1996 Reserve Forces Almanac.* (Falls Church, VA: Reserve Forces Almanac, 1996), 63.
2. USAR, *What's Next?*, 6.

· 8 ·

THE ROLE OF FAITH IN YOUR PREPARATION

One element of family life that gives security to families is the nurturing of their religious faith. Establishing a routine of attending your place of worship, Sunday school or CCD, and holding devotional time or Bible study helps in that nurturing process. If the family does these things regularly, when Dad has to leave for a deployment the church community will still be a part of the family's life, and it is likely to provide comfort and support in his absence.

Many military families say that religious faith enables them to keep a more positive attitude and that military separations become opportunities for growth and experiencing God's care in a more intimate way. Some people find themselves moving toward faith for the first time when deployment affects their lives. After Madeline Bentley's husband was deployed to Bosnia she said, "I do know that this agnostic is going to get down on her knees every night and pray to God for the safe return of not just my husband but of every man and woman serving over there."[1] She found herself naturally turning to God for help when she faced a family separation.

Individuals may find reassurance in their faith when they face the challenges of the military lifestyle. "I often wrestle with the natural conflict between my calling to be a military man and my calling to be a Christian husband and father. Yet I continue to see

that the Lord has given me a calling to do both well. I have decided
that the best thing I can do as a military man who feels called by
God to 'stay with it,' is to look for other ways in which I can minister to my wife and family rather than to be frustrated by the ways
in which I can't."[2] You can look to your faith for strength and
decide that you will have the same positive outlook.

If you have questions about faith or God, go to your chaplain or
spiritual leader and look for answers. The more answers you can
find to your questions before you face trials, the stronger you will be
when you find yourself tried. When you face hardship, you may still
find yourself asking why, but you'll have the security of your faith in
God and the knowledge that He is with you through it.

Many Active Duty military members and their families worship at military chapels. You may decide to turn to your chapel
community for support and the chaplains for help during family
separations. Most chaplains would be happy to counsel with you
and help you with spiritual needs as well as other difficulties. Remember that your chaplain can help you even if he or she isn't the
individual you want to counsel with. He or she understands the
military system and knows what it has to offer to solve your problems or meet your needs. In addition, chaplains are always ready
to refer you to competent civilians in whom they have confidence.
During times of mass deployment of personnel, there may not be
enough chaplains or military professionals available to meet the
needs of all of the families that are affected. Civilian churches,
hospitals, counseling centers, and service organizations work hard
to provide care to military families during times like this. Be aware
of the support networks available to you during the separations
you face and take full advantage of them for your family.

1. Bently, Madeline. "Praying for Safe Return." *The Stars and Stripes,* Euro-
     pean Edition, 31 December 1995: 16.
2. McColl, *Footsteps,* 109.

· 9 ·

CASUALTY PLANNING

If the military member doesn't return, the difficult decisions that the family will be faced with will be easier to make if you plan for them before you leave. The military helps you begin the process by urging every service member to have an updated will before deployment. You can also make plans to enable your wishes to be carried out and to ease responsibilities for your survivors. Discuss your ideas with your family and consult your legal office for information about how to make your plan most effective. You may want to consider the following:

- Where do you want to be buried? Are you eligible for burial in a national military cemetery and, if you are, do you want to be buried there?
- Do you own a cemetery plot? Where is it located? Where do you keep the deed?
- Where do you keep your will? The original should be located in a place where it would be easily found if you died and someone had to look for it. You may want to give a copy of your will to the person you name as your executor and to your closest relatives, who would likely be notified first if you died.

- Where do you keep guardianship papers or instructions for the care of your dependent children, if that isn't included in your will?
- Where would your family choose to live if you were killed? If you live in military housing, they would have limited time to make that decision.
- Where do you keep life insurance policies and other documents that need to be available in the event of your death? Does your family know what insurance policies you have?

As you plan for the possibility of a casualty, refer to the section of this book entitled "Some Don't Return" for ideas to help you understand what is involved in dealing with grief and funeral planning and how death notification is made. You can also ask your military Casualty Assistance office how you can prepare for the possibility of your death, to assist your family's decision-making process during the shock of death notification and funeral preparations.

· 10 ·

RESOURCES TO HELP YOU
PREPARE FOR SEPARATION

RESOURCES FOR SPOUSES AT HOME

- *Service Separations: A Wife's Perspective*
  by Beverly Moritz
  Available from: Focus on the Family
                      8605 Explorer Dr.
                      Colorado Springs, CO 80995
                      (800) 424-1984
                      www.family.org

  and: Officer's Christian Fellowship
                      3784 South Inca
                      Englewood, CO 80110
                      e-mail: ocfdenver@ocfhg.org
                      www.gospelcom.net/ocf

- *The Woman's Guide to Staying Safe*
  by Cheryl Reimold

- **Published by Channing L. Bete Co.:**
  Make the Most of Family Support Groups
  Preparing for Mobilization
  Family Support Groups
  Transition and the Family
  Living in a Military Family
  Military Family Life
  Available from your Family Support Center, your chaplain, or
  the publisher:
  Scriptographic Booklets
  Channing L. Bete Co. Inc.
  200 State Road
  South Deerfield, MA 01373-0200
  (800) 477-4776
  e-mail: custsvcs@channing-bete.com
  www.channing-bete.com

- *Today's Military Wife: Meeting the Challenges of Service Life*
  by Lydia Sloan Cline
  Available at bookstores; published by: Stackpole Books.

- *Heroes At Home: Help & Hope for America's Military Families*
  by Ellie Kay

RESOURCES FOR FAMILIES

- **Web sites operated by the National Institute for Building Long
  Distance Relationships**
  All of these web sites have great links, ideas, and information.

  www.daads.com
  Dads at a Distance—helps fathers who are away from their
  children maintain and strengthen their relationships during
  their absence.

www.momsovermiles.com
Moms Over Miles—helps mothers who have to be away to maintain and strengthen the relationships they have with their children while they're gone.

www.longdistancecouples.com
Long Distance Couples—helps couples maintain relationships with each other when they're separated.

www.longdistancegrandparenting.com
Grandparenting from a Distance.

- **Published by The Bureau For At-Risk Youth:**
  Titles in the Family Forum Library—Military Edition:
  Deployment and Reunion: Challenges and Opportunities
  Stress and the Military Family
  Loss and Change in the Military Family
  Communication Skills for the Military Family
  The Military Lifestyle and Children
  Family Readiness
  How to Be a Successful Young Military Family
  Helping Children Cope With Change
  The Single Military Parent

Available from your Family Support Center, your chaplain, or the publisher:
  The Bureau For At-Risk Youth
  135 Dupont Street
  P.O. Box 760
  Plainview, NY 11803-0760
  (800) 99-YOUTH
  e-mail: info@at-risk.com
  www.at-risk.com

- **Published by Channing L. Bete Co.:**
  Until Your Parent Comes Home Again; a coloring and
      activities book about deployment
  Military Families Are Special; a coloring and activities book
  Transition and the Family
  Preparing for Mobilization
  About Deployment
  Let's Talk About Deployment; an information and activities
      book
  Deployment Days; a coloring calendar for military families
  Write From the Heart; stationary kits for children
  Meeting the Challenges of Deployment
  Family Budgeting
  Checking Accounts
  Good Money Management For Military Personnel
  Credit Management For Military Personnel
  Beat the High Cost of Living
  Why You Should Have a Will
  Parents and Stress
  Disciplining Your Child
  Stress and Your Child
  Being a Father
  MISSION: READINESS: A Personal and Family Guide
  Available from your Family Support Center, your chaplain or
  the publisher:
  Scriptographic Booklets
  Channing L. Bete Co. Inc.
  200 State Road
  South Deerfield, MA 01373-0200
  (800) 477-4776
  e-mail: custsvcs@channing-bete.com
  www.channing-bete.com

- *Dare to Discipline*
  Bringing Up Boys
  by Dr. James Dobson

- *Withhold Not Correction*
  by Bruce Ray

- *101 Ways to Be A Long-Distance Super Dad . . . or Mom, Too!*
  by George Newman
  Available from:
      Blossom Valley Press
      5141 E. Woodgate
      P.O. Box 13378
      Tucson, AZ 85732-3378
      phone: (520) 325-1224

- **"The Military Father: Good Servicemen Can be Good Daddies too"**
  by F. Sitler
  The Navy Times Magazine, February 1, 1982, pages 28–30.
  Available in many libraries.

- **"Where's Papa?—How to Deal With Children When Daddy Goes Away"**
  by M. Lester
  The Navy Times Magazine, February 1, 1982, pages 32–33.
  Available in many libraries.

RESOURCES FOR SINGLE PARENTS

- **Published by The Bureau For At-Risk Youth:**
  From the Family Forum Library—Military Edition:
      The Single Military Parent
      How to be a Confident Single Parent
  From the Need to Know Library:
      Living With a Single Parent
  Titles offered under For Teens Only—Military Edition:
      Your Special Responsibilities and Benefits
      It's Time to Move Again

Making the Most of the Military Lifestyle
Where to Turn For Guidance and Support
Adjusting to Your New School
Appreciating Diversity in the Military
Challenges of Living in a Single-Parent Family
Available from your Family Support Center, your chaplain, or
the publisher:
The Bureau For At-Risk Youth
135 Dupont Street
P.O. Box 760
Plainview, NY 11803-0760
(800) 99-YOUTH
e-mail: info@at-risk.com
www.at-risk.com

- **Published by Channing L. Bete Co.:**
  Until Your Parent Comes Home Again; a coloring and activi-
      ties book about deployment
  Single Parenting
  About Family Care Plans
  Protect Your Family With a Family Care Plan
  Let's Talk About Deployment; an information and activities
      book
  About Being A Guardian For a Military Family Member
  Guardians for Military Members
Available from your Family Support Center, your chaplain, or
the publisher:
Scriptographic Booklets
Channing L. Bete Co. Inc.
200 State Road
South Deerfield, MA 01373-0200
(800) 477-4776

- *Single-Parent Family*
A monthly insert to the *Focus on the Family Magazine,* avail-
able from your chaplain or the publisher:
Single-Parent Family edition of *Focus on the Family Magazine*

8605 Explorer Drive
Colorado Springs, CO 80995
(800) 424-1984
www.family.org

- **Parents Without Partners**
1650 South Dixie Highway, Suite 510
Boca Raton, FL 33432
(561) 391-8833
www.parentswithoutpartners.org
This organization is international and offers discussion groups, workshops, and publications. They teach practical parenting and help single parents learn how to be alone without being lonely, how to communicate more effectively, and how to enjoy life as a single parent.

RESOURCES TO HELP CHILDREN

- *Saying Goodbye When You Don't Want To*
Teens Dealing With Loss
by Martha Bolton

- **Published by The Bureau For At-Risk Youth:**
Titles from the For Parents Only Series:
    Dealing With Your Child's Feelings
    Encouraging a Positive Attitude
    Teaching Your Child the Value of Friendship
    Teaching Your Child to Appreciate Diversity
    Building Positive Parent/Child Communication
    Teaching Your Child to Make Smart Choices
    Getting Along Better with Your Child
    Keeping Your Child Drug-Free
    Building Your Child's Self-Esteem
    Teaching Conflict Resolution Skills

Teaching Your Child Responsibility
Motivating Your Child to Success
Coloring Books:
  I'll Miss You
  I'm Proud to be a Military Kid
Available from your Family Support Center, your chaplain, or
the publisher:
  The Bureau For At-Risk Youth
  135 Dupont Street
  P.O. Box 760
  Plainview, NY 11803-0760
  (800) 99-YOUTH
  e-mail: info@at-risk.com
  www.at-risk.com

• **The Business Traveling Parent**
  How to stay close to your kids When You're Far Away
  by Dan Verdick
  Published by: Robins Lane Press
                 Beltsville, MD
                 www.robinslane.com
  Available at bookstores. If the bookstore near you does not have
  it, ask them to order it.

• *Memories of Me,* for children ages 4–12
  WriteBack Mail
  The letter-writing kits include stationery, envelopes, calendars,
  and stickers, and are available in Standard or Military versions.
  They also offer a letter-writing idea book and craft projects.
  These resources may be available at your Family Support Cen-
  ter, or you can contact the publisher:
  The Write Connection Co.
  Letter Writing Program
  P.O. Box 293
  Lake Forest, CA 92630
  (714) 581-3283
  (800) 334-3143
  Fax (714) 859-0405

- **Published by Channing L. Bete Co.:**
    What You Should Know About Stress and Your Child
    Until Your Parent Comes Home Again; a coloring and
        activities book about deployment
    Military Families Are Special; a coloring and activities book
    Let's Talk About Deployment; an information and activities
        book
    Deployment Days; a coloring calendar for military families
    Disciplining Your Child
    Stress and Your Child
    Being a Father
Available from your Family Support Center, your chaplain or
the publisher:
    Scriptographic Booklets
    Channing L. Bete Co. Inc.
    200 State Road
    South Deerfield, MA 01373-0200
    (800) 477-4776
    e-mail: custsvcs@channing-bete.com
    www.channing-bete.com

Help for Children from Libraries

- Any library has books to help children understand family sepa-
    ration. Ask your librarian to help you find them. Here are a few
    titles to get you started:
    Books at the Juvenile Level:
        Surviving Your Parent's Divorce, by Charles Boeckman (see
            chapter 3, "What to Do About Your Own Feelings")
        Coping When Your Family Falls Apart, by Dianna Daniels
            Booher (see chapter 7, "How to Cope")
        *Everything You Need to Know about Living with a Single
        Parent,* by Richard E. Mancini
    For Younger Children:
        Don't You Know There's a War on?, by James Stevenson
        I Love My Mother, by Paul Zindel
        Will You Count the Stars Without Me?, by Jane Breskin Zalben

The Terrible Thing That Happened at Our House, by Marge
  Blaine
Will Dad Ever Move Back Home, by Paula Hogan
The Giving Tree, by Shel Silverstein
The Goodbye Painting, by Linda Berman

ARMY RESOURCES

- **Army Family Team Building**
  Army Family Team Building (AFTB) is a program to train military members and their families and help prepare them for family separations. It is used by both Active Duty and Reserve
  components.
  AFTB Office
  U. S. Army Community and Family Support Center
  ATTN: CFSC-FST (AFTB)
  4700 King Street
  Alexandria, VA 22302-4418
  (703) 681-7401
  http://trol.redstone.army.mil/mwr/aftb

AIR FORCE RESOURCES

- **Ombudsmen**
  The Air Force has an ombudsman program to help families
  with deployments. The ombudsman is an Active Duty member, spouse, or family support expert chosen by the Wing Commander. Like the Navy ombudsmen, those in the Air Force are
  not there to solve problems, but to help families find resources
  as a liaison between the families and command. To find out if
  there is an ombudsman on your base, contact your Family Support Center.

- **Family Readiness NCO**
  The Air Force has appointed and trained Active Duty NCOs to work at the Family Support Centers to meet the needs of families of deployed personnel. They coordinate with other caregivers on base to hold support group meetings and help ease the stress of separation. They can be effective advocates for families, and some have videophones available for family use to keep in touch with the deployed member. Contact your Family Support Center to see what resources are available at your base.

- **Air Force Internet Web Page**
  The Air Force has a Web page called Crossroads: AFCROSSROADS.COM
  This site will give you information about all DOD installations, and also has an Air Force Spouse Forum. The Forum is designed specifically for spouses, to provide communication on a variety of Air Force issues, and to assist them during times of military duty that result in family separation. Spouses can post messages and participate in the following manner:
  > Within the Crossroads site, click on the category entitled "Spouse Network."
  > Register as a new user, creating your own user name and password.
  > You will receive an e-mail verifying your approval (usually within about 5 minutes). Once approved, you can sign in and access the Spouse Forum.

Don't be worried about having to provide your Social Security Number, full name, birth date, and personal e-mail address to access sections of this Web site. The information is verified through the DEERS records to be sure each user is authorized, and is submitted using Secure Socket Layer (SSL) encryption in order to provide the best security available and honor the privacy act. Remember that if DEERS does not have correct information, you will be denied access to the password-protected sections of Crossroads. You may want to check to be sure your DEERS records are accurate.

Navy Resources

- *Daddy's Days Away*; a deployment activity book for parents and children.

- *Navy Family Deployment Guide*
Ask your Navy Family Services Center for the guide or call one of these numbers: (800) FSC-LINE or (757) 444-6289.

- **Naval Services FamilyLine / LIFELines Network**
Naval Services FamilyLine was formerly known as The Navy Wifeline Association. It is a volunteer informational and educational organization that acquaints families with sea service traditions and helps spouses cope with special problems brought about because of deployment. The Naval Services FamilyLine has an extensive web site.

  Access it at www.lifelines2000.org / familyline. From the homepage you may want to begin by clicking on "Welcome Aboard." There are links to several topics. For information write:
  The Naval Services FamilyLine
  Washington Navy Yard, Building 172
  1254 9th Street SE, Suite 104
  Washington DC 20374-5067
  Phone: DSN 288-2333
         Commercial (202) 433-2333
  Office hours: M–F 10AM–1PM EST / EDT

Navy Programs and Workshops

- **Couples Pre-Deployment**
Couples Pre-Deployment prepares couples for the emotional cycles of deployment. Suggestions are given for ways to cope, communicate, and keep connected while apart. It's usually presented two months to one week before departure.

- **Singles at Sea**
  Single sailors are informed about financial issues, maintaining communication with family and friends, planning for reunion, and learning how to make the most of the deployment. This program is usually presented two months to one week before departure.

- **Financial Planning For Deployment**
  Financial issues are examined, including budgets, allotments, savings, bills, powers of attorney, and wills. This program is sometimes presented with the Couples Pre-Deployment Program or Singles at Sea Program, and sometimes as early as five months before the deployment.

- **Parent/Child Pre-Deployment**
  Parent/Child Pre-Deployment prepares parents and children to cope with confusion and anxiety related to the deployment. During the parents' meeting, the children participate in age-specific planned activities that are supervised by trained Navy Family Support Center Staff members. The program sometimes includes a puppet show to help children learn how to deal with their worry about the deployment, and is presented during the two months to one week leading up to departure.

MARINE CORPS RESOURCES

- *What's Next?: A Guide to Family Readiness for the U. S. Marine Corps* (includes helpful checklists and forms)
  Available from your Family Services Center.

RESERVE AND GUARD RESOURCES

- **Guide to Reserve Family Member Benefits**
  Available from your Family Support Center or on the Reserve
  Affairs home page: http://raweb.osd.mil/publications/index.htm

- **Published by Channing L. Bete Co.:**
  About Preparing for Mobilization
  Meeting the Challenges of Deployment
  About Family Care Plans
  Protect Your Family With a Family Care Plan
  Make the Most of Family Support Groups
  Family Support Groups
  Available from your Family Support Center, your chaplain, or
  the publisher:
  Scriptographic Booklets
  Channing L. Bete Co. Inc.
  200 State Road
  South Deerfield, MA 01373-0200
  (800) 477-4776
  e-mail: custsvcs@channing-bete.com
  www.channing-bete.com

ARMY RESERVE RESOURCES

- *What's Next?: A Guide to Family Readiness for the Army Reserve* (includes helpful checklists and forms)
  Available from your Family Support Center.

- **Family Readiness Online**
  The Army Reserve offers family support programs to help families prepare for deployments. Many of these programs are courses that are part of the Army Family Team Building Program. Operation Ready is also available to specifically address

readiness for families. To access information online, look at: trol.redstone.army.mil/acslink

- **Army Reserve Headquarters Hotline**
  (800) 359-8483 ext. 464-8995/8947

AIR FORCE RESERVE RESOURCES

- **Air Reserve Headquarters Hotline**
  (800) 223-1784 ext. 71294

COAST GUARD RESERVE RESOURCES

- **Coast Guard Reserve Web Site**
  Access the web site at www.uscg.mil.
  Users should click on Reserve information.

RESOURCES FOR PEOPLE SUPPORTING AND SERVING MILITARY FAMILIES

- **Published by Channing L. Bete Co.:**
  About Being A Guardian For a Military Family Member
  About Family Support Groups
  Family Budgeting
  Checking Accounts
  Good Money Management For Military Personnel
  Why You Should Have a Will
  Available from your Family Support Center, your chaplain, or the publisher:

Scriptographic Booklets
Channing L. Bete Co. Inc.
200 State Road
South Deerfield, MA 01373-0200
(800) 477-4776
e-mail: custsvcs@channing-bete.com
www.channing-bete.com

• *Caring For Military Families: Facing Separation, War, and Homecoming*
by David A. Paap
Order from: Stephen Ministries
              2045 Innerbelt Business Center Drive
              St. Louis, MO 63114-5765
              (314) 428-2600
              www.stephenministries.com

• **Parents Away Group**
Laurel Bay Schools in Laurel Bay, South Carolina, have a program they call Parents Away Group. The school counselors present the idea to children at the beginning of each school year, asking how many parents are deployed or away from their families. They send a letter home with the children, explaining the support group and giving the parents or caregivers the opportunity to allow the children to participate.

At the support group meetings, children are encouraged to bring family pictures, postcards, presents from the absent parent, or talk about special activities the family is involved in. The structure of the group varies, but the objectives are to help the children realize they are important members of their families, to promote sharing and expressing their feelings, and to provide activities that will help children communicate with the absent parent. Counselors may use world maps or globes to show each child where their parent is in relationship to where they are. They may even take group pictures to send to parents.

You may want to begin a group similar to Parents Away Group in your community if there is no support group for children in your area.

- *While You Are Away*
  by Norma Kimrey Colwell
  illustrated by Gloria Sallings
  While You Are Away can be used to help pre-kindergarten through 6th grade students with temporary family separation. The program contains session plans and activities that can be used with individuals or small groups. (It is used by Parents Away Group, listed above.) To order, contact the publisher and ask for *While You Are Away* (order # WA910):
  MAR*CO Products, Inc.
  Department S97
  1443 Old York Road
  Warminster, PA 18974
  Phone: (800) 448-2197 (Monday-Friday)
  Fax: (215) 956-9041

- *Military Family Resource Center*
  Military Family Resource Center
  CS4, Suite 302, Room 309
  1745 Jefferson Davis Highway
  Arlington, VA 22202-3424
  Phone: Commercial: (703) 602-4964
            DSN: 332-4964
  www.mfrc.calib.com/
  The Military Family Resource Center is an invaluable tool for helping military families. They have a wide variety of web sites and programs to provide help, referral and information. The web sites they run include *Military Children and Youth, Military Family Week, Parenting Initiatives, Child Abuse Prevention,* and many more special issues. Visit their web sites to research how they address topics of interest to you or your organizations. To contact an Information Specialist regarding any of their services write or call:

Military Family Resource Center
4040 North Fairfax Drive, Room 420
Arlington, VA 22203-1635
Phone: DSN: 426-9053
        Commercial: (703) 696-9053
Fax: DSN: 426-9053
        Commercial: (703) 696-9062
e-mail: mfrc@hq.odedodea.edu

• *Working with Military Children—A Primer For School Personnel*
  by the Virginia Joint Military Family Services Board
  Distributed by
      Military Family Clearinghouse
  4015 Wilson Boulevard, Suite 903
  Arlington, VA 22203-5190
  (703) 696-5806
  DSN: 426-5806
This publication is targeted for school staff, and guidance counselors in particular. It addresses the role schools play in supporting the children of military service members. It includes
an activities section for teachers to use with individual children or in groups.

II

DEPLOYMENT

· 1 ·

SURVIVING SHOCK

It was a warm August afternoon and I was still in shock emotionally. I wanted to write Ren a letter but wasn't sure where to begin. How do you start a letter to your husband when he was jerked away from you on a two-hour notice without warning? He left for a classified location and didn't even have an address to give me.

As I sat and thought about what to write, I wanted to tell him how upset I was that he was sent away so suddenly and unmercifully. If only we had been warned about what to expect. My mind wandered through a lot of "what if's" and "if only's."

Ren had been gone for two weeks and finally called me to give me an address. The phone call was so short I'll always remember every word:

"Let me quick give you this address so you know where to send mail, and then if we're cut off, you'll have it . . ."

I scribbled it down as fast as he could dictate it to me, and then the phone line went dead. The 90-second phone call was over.

"At least now I have some connection to him," I thought. I decided I'd write every day until he was on his way home. I didn't dare to think about how long that would be.

I began the letter by telling him how glad I was to hear his voice on the phone and to know he had arrived safely at his destination. I told him all I could remember about what we did during the past two weeks. Dan and I had just returned from Michigan. I had mixed feelings about writing about our visit with the Dutch relatives because Ren looked forward to seeing them and I knew he felt bad about missing their visit. But I was determined to include him in all we did, so I told him all about the visit. He missed enough by not being there in person, I reasoned; I'd do whatever I could to help him visualize it. (He later told me that it meant a lot to him to hear about our trip.)

My emotions were on a roller coaster as I wrote that first letter. I had so many questions that couldn't be answered: "Will there be a war?" "How long will Ren be gone?" "Will he stay where he is, or be moved to another location?" "If this is military life, do we still want to make it a career?"

The last question was the only one I could answer with certainty. Yes! We loved the military lifestyle and knew that separations could come. I dreaded the prospect of being separated, but now that he was deployed I knew there would be faith and strength to endure. God called Ren to be a military chaplain and I knew He would take care of our family, each in our separate locations.

All of the local radio and TV stations wanted to talk to Desert Shield families. A TV station called me to request an interview. I was repulsed by the negative attitudes being shown on TV interviews and said no. Many of the wives that were interviewed behaved as if they didn't realize their husbands could be called on for military action and they were bitter about the deployment. As I wrote to tell Ren about it, I thought about the request I had turned down and decided I'd say "yes" if I were asked again. (I was.) Maybe I could show a healthy and positive attitude in spite of the uncertain circumstances. (I did.) I wrote everything I was thinking.

After I finished the letter, I walked to the post office to mail my ten-page first communication to my husband. I still didn't look forward to the separation, but I felt a change in my emotional response to it. Looking backward, I realize I was coming out of my phase of shock and beginning to mentally plan how I would endure.

I would take one day at a time and keep a positive attitude. For mutual support, I decided to look for other wives whose husbands were gone. Shared time would be more pleasant and move faster than time alone. I'd go to the base support meetings every week, too. The more I thought about it, the more I began to believe Dan and I could make it through the separation.

· 2 ·
PRAYER POEMS FROM A WIFE'S HEART

MOTHER'S VISIT

by Beth Blase

There she is, Lord,
Hallelujah!
You've brought her safely
Through ice and snow.
She looks terrific
At seventy-four.
She insists on relieving me
Of some of these responsibilities
For a spell.
She has a story
That outdoes any predicament
I've been in this year.
How she makes me laugh!
Lord, she has a great appreciation
For where I'm at.

She was thirty years a military wife.
She was often single-handed
"Holding down the fort."
Next to You, Lord,
She's the only one
Who understands me right now.
Thank You so much
For her friendship
And her rescue. *

*Both poems used by permission.

FRUSTRATION

by Beth Blase

The car won't start
The dog won't wait
The baby won't stop
The phone keeps ringing
The toilet keeps running
The moths are everywhere
The toys are everywhere
The frig is empty
The dryer is full
The yard needs mowing
My hair needs washing
My daughter needs money
My purse is missing
My son is missing
Hold Everything!
Lord, I give my exasperation to You,
For you are sufficient
I will not give up,
I will give thanks!
Because for all of these situations
You, my God, are able
"to make all grace abound
Toward me,
Always having all sufficiency
In all things"
So that I might have
An abundance of Your grace
For every good work.**

(Meditation verse: II Corinthians 9:8)

· 3 ·

GOING, GONE

Family separations are a fact of life in the military. With smaller amounts of personnel to draw from, everyone has to take a turn being deployed, probably more than once. You may receive notification of deployment months, weeks, or days ahead of your expected departure. On the other hand, you could have only hours or minutes to prepare.

Whatever amount of notification you receive, the effect is that the family is separated and must adjust to this change in their lives. "When that last olive-drab truck full of soldiers roars down the dirt road to an unnamed field site, or that Navy ship shoves out to sea for an extended deployment,"[1] or the one you love boards the plane for other parts of the world, "many a military spouse left behind to juggle the household begins to wonder what malicious schemes Murphy's Law has in store for her."[2] Military wives know that whenever their husbands are gone repairs need to be made or children have accidents. But if the family prepares for separation, the wife will have no reason to fear even though she may still feel the shock of a sudden separation, because she knows what to do and where to find help.

The shock may take days or weeks to subside. Shock at a time of change is not something that should be seen as weakness;

THE MILITARY WIFE'S FAMILY SEPARATION GEAR

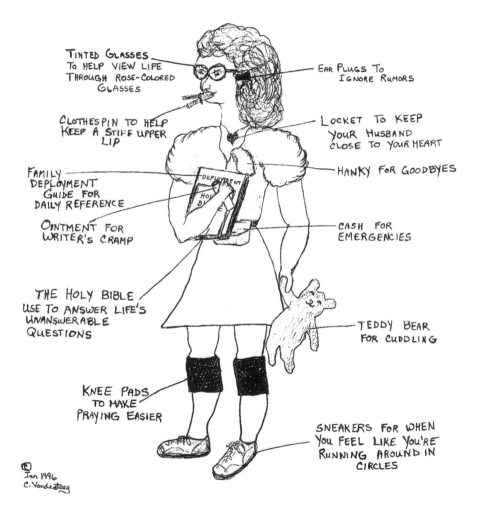

TINTED GLASSES TO HELP VIEW LIFE THROUGH ROSE-COLORED GLASSES

EAR PLUGS TO IGNORE RUMORS

CLOTHESPIN TO HELP KEEP A STIFF UPPER LIP

LOCKET TO KEEP YOUR HUSBAND CLOSE TO YOUR HEART

FAMILY DEPLOYMENT GUIDE FOR DAILY REFERENCE

HANKY FOR GOODBYES

OINTMENT FOR WRITER'S CRAMP

CASH FOR EMERGENCIES

THE HOLY BIBLE USE TO ANSWER LIFE'S UNANSWERABLE QUESTIONS

TEDDY BEAR FOR CUDDLING

KNEE PADS TO MAKE PRAYING EASIER

SNEAKERS FOR WHEN YOU FEEL LIKE YOU'RE RUNNING AROUND IN CIRCLES

© Jan 1996
C. Vandesteeg

instead, it should be viewed as a natural part of the body's emotional response to change, that enables wives whose husbands are deployed to adjust to the change and to "'catch up' emotionally with what they already understand intellectually."[3] Facing these feelings and recognizing them as understandable under the circumstances helps wives feel emotional health instead of a loss of their faculties. Fears are minimized and they can carry on with life more effectively.

When It's Time to Say Goodbye

When the day of departure comes, each family must decide who will go to see Dad leave. Some families say it's easier to watch him go together, even though the parting may be emotional. Whatever you decide, it's important for each family member to say goodbye individually.

Many wives feel a sense of relief once the goodbyes are finished. That can be especially true for families who receive notification months or weeks before departure. They've anticipated the pain of separating, and waiting for it to happen can seem as unpleasant as the separation itself. Relief from the pain of saying goodbye is met with the challenge of going on with life at home without Dad.

Your family may find it easier to leave the departure location if you have an activity planned or something special to do. Depending on the ages of your children and their interests, you may want to go to the zoo or a park, or go to the mall. When my husband left on short notice, our 16-year-old son and I went to McDonald's, and then to register him for school, since it happened to be our assigned day to do that. It gave us an empty feeling to see my husband leave suddenly, but going to school cemented into our consciousness that we had to go on with life on our own. It was a good beginning for us because we were immediately brought into a routine that we would have followed even without the separation.

When you face family separation, think of routine things that have to be done as a way to help you get on track and survive the time apart. Recognize that the separation demands some adjustment, but your family life can stay remarkably similar to your regular routine while you incorporate the necessary changes. Expect to miss your husband and have times of loneliness, but also expect that the time apart will be a time of growth and drawing closer to each other in new ways. Many women say that separations help them learn to be more independent and give them confidence that they can handle more at home than they thought they could.

1. Krajeski, Margaret. "Keeping it Together When You're Apart," in *Married to the Military,* Supplement to *Army Times, Navy Times,* and *Air Force Times,* ed. Margaret Roth, 16 May 1994: 46.
2. Ibid.
3. Paap, David A. *Caring For Military Families.* (St. Louis, MO: Stephen Ministries, 1991), 19.

· 4 ·

TIPS FOR DEPLOYED PARENTS

There are a number of things you can do to show love and care to your family while you're separated from them. Let them know you've arrived at your location safely. Communicate often with them. Write your family letters and tell them as much as you can about where you're living and what you're doing. Give them an idea of what a day is usually like for you there. Any details you can share with them will help them visualize you in your surroundings and feel like they have a tangible connection with you. If there are brochures of sightseeing attractions or literature about the area where you are deployed, send them to your family. If it's possible, take pictures to send home. You may find that keeping a calendar diary is a good way to communicate with your family. Write on a calendar at least one thing you did that day, and at the end of the month send the page to your family.

COMMUNICATING WITH CHILDREN

Children enjoy receiving small souvenirs, patches, bumper stickers, buttons, stamps, shells, rocks, leaves, flowers, or pictures from Dad. You may want to make up games to send your children in the mail. For example, you could make a word search puzzle, with a list of words, and see how many your children can find. Maybe you'd like to play chess by mail with older children, each of you getting one move per letter. Games may stretch out over a long time, but they add anticipation to writing and receiving letters.

Children like to share special secrets with their parents, and you can incorporate a sense of personal connection to your children by finding unique ways to communicate with each of them. You may want to work out a special code, assigning a different letter to each letter of the alphabet, so when you write a message in code only the child with the key can interpret the message. For example, *Q RQPP LAM* says *I MISS YOU*. If you keep a record of the key and send one to your child, you can use the same code throughout the deployment. You can develop a different code and key for each child.

Some children enjoy getting multiple-choice letters. For example, you could write the following:

Dear Bobby,

Today I was (a) thinking, (b) singing, (c) sulking, or, (d) dreaming about you. You were (a) in school, (b) at home, or, (c) at the zoo with me and we were looking at (a) pictures, (b) your math homework, (c) the rain, or, (d) a zebra.

Love, (a) your Dad, (b) King Kong, or, (c) grandma.

You could put the answers on the back of the page: *answers: a,c,d,a*

Variations of the multiple-choice letters could be true/false test formats. Ask your child which of two foods is better, or what activity is more fun to participate in or to watch. Filling in the blank questions could also be a fun way to get your children to tell you their favorite classes in school, or favorite television shows. Use your imagination to tailor ideas to each child.

You may already be close to your children, but as they grow, they change, and innovative letter writing while you're away can help you keep up with subtle changes as they occur, as well as make letter-writing fun. The way you choose to do that will depend on your children's preferences and your own. Try to think like each child does to help you decide what type of communication to use.

Children appreciate mail of their own from Dad; they love to see their names on an envelope or postcard. Depending on your children's ages, you might want to use stickers, colored paper or pens, or different types of lettering when you write to them. You might want to share in your letters to your children that you miss them but since you can't be there right now, you're glad you can at least write to them. If you express some of your feelings to them, it will be easier for them to sort through and talk about their feelings. When you write to them, encourage your children to write back to you by telling them what you enjoyed from their last letters, and compliment them for writing good letters to you.

You may want to ask your children to tell you how your favorite sports teams are doing and make a game of guessing which teams will win certain games or championships. Don't forget to ask them to tell you about games they may be playing, too. Maybe your children aren't involved in sports, but play the piano or another instrument, or take art, ballet, or singing lessons. Ask them what they are involved in, what they enjoy about it, and how they're progressing.

If you have trouble coming up with ideas, *The Business Traveling Parent,* by Dan Verdick, suggests over one hundred ways for parents to stay close to their children when they're separated. Mr. Verdick includes activities to do with your children before you leave, while you're gone, and when you get back home. He also gives resources to expand on some of his ideas. His book is available at most bookstores, and is worth asking for, even if the store has to order it for you.

· 5 ·

COMMUNICATION FROM A
DISTANCE

An important way to nurture your marriage is to communicate freely and often. One of the best ways to do that from a distance is by letter. Some families find it helpful to date their letters or mark them with a small number somewhere on the envelope so the person receiving it will know which letter was written first if they are received out of order, which you should expect during most deployments. Others like to communicate by telephone or E-mail. Depending on the deployed location, telephone calls and the use of the Internet may or may not be possible. If telephones are available, remember that calls are likely to be very costly, so keep them within the budget of your family.

PHONE

Phone calls can be disappointing because each spouse is so excited to hear the other's voice that they hardly know what to say. After the phone call, they may spend the whole day thinking about everything they wish they would have said. So if you decide to communicate by phone, you may want to try to make a list of things to talk about before your call. As you go through each day and think of something to share with your husband or to ask him, write it down. Then you can refer to your notes when the phone rings or when you write your next letter.

Keeping a list of things to communicate is a good way to remember to share details about the family's activities with your husband and for your husband to share his life with his family at home. Lists may seem cumbersome, but they will help you communicate more of yourself to your spouse while you are separated. If you can avoid writing to your husband or speaking on the phone when you feel down or frustrated, you will also be able to communicate better. During those times you aren't your true self, and later you would probably regret something you said or the way you said it.

TAPE RECORDERS AND VIDEOTAPES

Exchanging tapes can be an inexpensive way to hear each other's voice without as much time-consciousness as may be necessary during phone calls. You may want to talk about the list of things you want to communicate to your husband, but have trouble knowing how to write and don't have time to talk about during phone calls. On tape, you can take time to describe details and talk about how you feel. You may want to give each child an opportunity to talk to Dad, or tape school programs or sporting events they are involved in for Dad. Of course, Dad must have a recorder or VCR available for his use.

E-MAIL

Computers are often available in deployed locations, so your family may have the option of communication by E-mail. Many people find it easier to send an E-mail than to write a letter, so they communicate more often by computer. Some family members send messages almost daily. That takes a lot of the pain out of the separation and keeps morale higher. Some units have computers that families of deployed individuals can use if they don't have one at home. Ask your unit whether E-mail will be available during your family's separation. Remember that E-mail is not a secure method of communication. Your message may be read by other people, so don't use it to talk about things you want kept private.

VIDEO LINKS

Videophones allow families to see and talk to each other from a distance. They can be hooked up to any phone system, and are used by military families when the components are available. This form of communication can be a mixed blessing, because some people say they miss each other more when they can see their loved one but cannot touch them or be near them. However, there is comfort in seeing first hand that family members in both locations are well, and the visual contact may help families envision the deployed member in his or her new surroundings. Ask your unit command or Family Support Center whether video links are available in your area.

MARS

An often unknown and less usual method of contact during deployments is MARS, the Military Affiliated Radio System. MARS operators are HAM radio owners who are certified by the Federal Communications Commission and meet the qualifications to participate in the MARS program. They are volunteers who try to provide a point of personal contact for service members and their families. MARS operators have a strict code of confidentiality. The MARS operators will call you to verify that they've reached the correct person, give you their name and location, tell you they are

MARS operators, and tell you who they are calling for. The operator will ask you whether you've talked on a patch phone; be sure you understand how to use it, because there is a delay between speaking and hearing, and you must say "over" when you want the other party to respond. The deployed person must initiate the call, and conditions must be just right for the calls to come through. These calls are billed as collect calls from wherever the MARS operator is located. So, while you can't rely on MARS calls for regular communication, they may provide a morale boost if they're available to you.

TELEGRAMS

Some families may want to send messages by Western Union during times of separation. Birthday, anniversary, or other special messages can be sent and received quickly. To ask for information or to send a message by Western Union, call (800) 325-6000.

LETTERS

When you write letters during deployments, remember that there are often mail delays in correspondence with locations outside the continental United States. Mail from either direction may be delivered in three or four days, or may take three or four weeks. So if you don't receive mail from your spouse for a week or two, that is not necessarily a sign that your partner isn't writing to you. You may receive four or five letters at once, and then have a week without mail. These delays can be frustrating, but if you expect them to occur you won't jump to the conclusion that your mate has forgotten you. In spite of mail delays, letters are a preferred way to communicate during separations.

Letters are a good means of communication because they can be read over and over again. Knowing that your husband may read your letter several times, write him the details of home life that you know he misses and will enjoy hearing. Express appreciation for something he mentioned in the last letter or package you received. Without becoming overly nostalgic, you can mention something in each letter that will remind your husband of a special memory you share, secrets between the two of you, or things that make you feel close to each other. It may help you write as if you are talking to your husband if you have a picture of him in front of you while you write your letter.

Try to encourage, rather than criticize, in your letters. Let your husband or wife know that you appreciate the way extra challenges are being met, whether at home or for the military mission. Even though you may be miles apart, you can still have meaningful communication. "The message that should come through loud and clear when a couple is apart is, 'You're my priority. You're important.'"[1] Try to communicate that priority by telling each other as much about what is happening in your lives as possible.

Don't be afraid to share feelings with each other in letters; share them openly and specifically. Try not to leave your husband wondering what you were trying to say. When you're sharing feelings in letters, don't assume you know what your husband means or try to read between the lines—if you aren't sure about what he's trying to say in his letter, ask questions or for more information in your next letter. Don't risk misunderstanding each other, but fear of misunderstanding should not prevent you from sharing from your heart in your letters. Many people discover that it is easier to write about their deepest feelings and thoughts than it is to talk about them.

It can also be difficult to share household problems when your husband is too far away to be able to help you. Try not to let your letters become negative when you write about family problems. If you prepared a *Family Deployment Guide* before the separation, you should have answers to most problems that would arise, or at least know who to call for help. Then, instead of writing to your husband about the problem when you feel helpless to deal with it, you may be able to write to him to share how you successfully solved the problem. Then you'll be able to tell him how happy you are to have the *Deployment Guide* you made together before he left, and he will be able to tell you how proud he is of the way you took care of the problem. He will be glad you are able to manage your household so well.

Our son, Dan, and I decided to help each other learn to drive my husband's stick-shift car after he deployed. We'd drive to a deserted area of the base in the evening as it was getting dark, and take turns driving until we both felt comfortable shifting without killing the engine or jerking the car. Then we decided it was test time, and one night we went to the commissary parking lot. The driveway to the parking lot was a steep hill, so we drove half way up, stopped, and tried to continue up the hill without rolling backward or killing the engine. It was a comical sight, I'm sure, and it took more than one night of practice, but we finally mastered it. We both felt good about our accomplishment, and my husband enjoyed getting letters telling him about our little driving classes.

You may decide to get a job while your husband is deployed. When you write, tell him where you work, what your job is like and what you do. Describe how you get there, what the building looks like, and what your work area is like. Then he can try to visualize you at work and will feel closer to you. You may enjoy keeping journals and sharing them with each other when he gets home. Maybe it would be fun to make up a questionnaire of thoughts you'd discuss if your husband were at home, and send it to him. Send him cards or letters you've received from friends that may not be writing to him at his deployed location.

INCLUDE THE CHILDREN

In addition to hearing from you, your husband wants to hear about and from your children. Pictures are a great way to show him your children's growth and interests. Encourage your children to write to Dad on a regular basis, maybe once a week or once every two weeks. Some families enjoy making a Sunday afternoon project out of writing to Dad, with everyone writing notes to put together in a family care package. If your family has a pet, Dad might enjoy hearing a story about the pet's activities that week. One of your children may want to write to Dad from the pet's point of view.

If you have small children or a baby born after Dad leaves home, he will want to keep up with each new stage the child grows through. In your letters, describe their looks, little things they do (pull on their toes, suck their thumb, twirl a strand of hair, comb Mom's hair, try on sunglasses, etc.) and their vocabulary development. Try to give Dad an idea of every child's growth, personality and interests, regardless of their age level. If you have a new baby, you might want to send him the baby's footprint or handprint periodically, or a strand of hair. Your communication to your husband about your children can take the form of journal entries; you can add ideas or things they've done as you think of them and mail an installment weekly.

Making Time to Communicate

The family at home and the deployed parent may each want to keep calendar diaries. The family can choose to keep one as a corporate project or each family member can keep a separate calendar. Use a calendar that has room to make a note each day or make your own calendars for each month. Each person can write at least one thing on their calendar before they go to bed each night. At the end of each month everyone can mail his or her calendar pages to Dad.

Don't write only once a week or once a month though. Think of your letters as your time together if he were at home, and talk to him by writing as much as you would if you were talking to him in person. Even if you do this carefully and tell him everything, you will find later that there are things you forgot to tell him and that he missed out on in your home life. We still discovered things my husband missed a year after he returned from being deployed, and while he was gone I wrote daily to be sure he didn't miss anything.

The more you share in letters about your daily lives, the easier it will be to understand each other when he gets back home.

Missing out on things that happen at home is inevitable because he is *NOT* there, but if you make a concentrated effort to communicate often you can minimize the strain of what is missed and make him feel like he is still included in the family. Send your husband news about the relatives, neighbors, and friends. (Of course, he can return the favor by telling you about his friends, what he does when he is not on duty, and how he feels about his work—anything that is on his mind.) You may want to send him clippings from the newspaper or a copy of his favorite magazine.

CARE PACKAGES

A care package is a good way to let him know he's loved and on your mind. Remember that his living space is probably limited, so it may be best to send him things that are disposable. Check with the Post Office to see whether there are any mailing restrictions before you prepare a package. There may be regulations about the size parcel you may send or about the contents you may include.

Care package items include spiral notebooks, paper, envelopes, stamps, pens, gum, candy, trail mix, a favorite snack food, taped TV shows, puzzles, games, music tapes or CDs, videotapes or DVDs, magazines, newspapers, comics, your child's artwork, aspirin, Tylenol, shampoo, toothpaste, toothbrush, soap, towels, new underwear or socks, family pictures, thumbtacks, tape, a few Christmas decorations, etc. Pack the box carefully, with enough paper that the contents don't shift when you tip the box, and use reinforced tape to seal the box. If you are sending a box for a special occasion, be sure to allow plenty of time for delivery if mail is slow.

If you send candy, cookies, or food that is not professionally sealed, ants may invade your package and enjoy your goodies before your husband gets it. I always wrap food in plastic wrap, and then insert it into a sealed baggie. If I have metal tins available, I put baggies of food inside the tins before mailing. Before I learned to do this, one Christmas we received a luscious-looking box of homemade fudge from some relatives—that was full of red ants. Our family made a joke out of it by saying that the communist ants had confiscated it, but we were sure disappointed to have to throw it away. Don't let that happen to any goodies you mail.

Be creative as you make care packages. You know what your husband enjoys. Let him know you are thinking of him and waiting for his return. He wants to know that he's missed, just like you want to know that he misses you. Do all you can to keep your husband involved in the family. Some families enjoy making a family newsletter to send to Dad. If there are grandparents, aunts, uncles, or cousins who are close, you may want to include them in your newsletter. Children may want to include news about school or other activities they participate in.

Enlist the help of your children in your effort to keep your husband informed. If decisions that affect them can wait until you hear from him again, ask your children to write and discuss it with Dad before you make the decision. Children of all ages can sense your attitude and will imitate, to some degree, your response to the separation. Think about the fact that you set the tone for your family's response to the separation. If you have an attitude that honestly communicates that "it hurts to be apart, but if we all stay positive we'll get through this and be able to handle whatever comes our way," you'll probably be surprised at how much easier it is to handle the daily trials you encounter.

1.   Doke, DeeDee. "Long-Distance Love: How to Keep Close When You're Far Apart." *The Stars and Stripes*, European Edition, 30 December 1995: 17.

· 6 ·

CARING FOR CHILDREN WHILE
A PARENT IS AWAY

Children don't have enough life experience to know how to react when a parent goes away for military duty. Research shows that the way children respond to family separation is probably connected to their sense of identity and how they relate to others instead of connection to the pain of saying goodbye to their parent. Children react to the stress at home caused by the separation, and specifically reflect their mother's reaction to their father's absence instead of their own grief that he's gone.

Children who have a strong bond with their father miss him more when he leaves, but recover faster.[1] Randall Lindsey, a professor at California State University at Los Angeles who specializes in education and outreach for at-risk youth, said, "Typically . . . younger children fare best during deployments—and the shorter the deployment, the better for all."[2] Lindsey agrees with other researchers in his emphasis on meeting the needs of families, as well as the mission, in planning deployments. If the needs of families are considered and an effort is made to help meet the needs, both the parents and the children will be able to cope with family separation more effectively.

Children usually look at their parents to learn how they should respond to the deployment. "Children will find their own way of coping. . . . The main influence on how well the children cope with the family separation is the attitude displayed both by the present parent and the absent one."[3] "If a separation is 'Mommy goes bonkers' time, the kids go bonkers, too. But if Mommy remains cool, the kids remain cool . . ."[4] How parents act during difficult times often teaches children more than what they say. If parents are positive and attentive to their children's responses to the changes, they can guide children through military separation with a minimum of difficulty.

A sensitive mother will tell her children's teachers that Dad just left, so the teachers will understand if there is a change in children's behavior or performance at school. Then teachers can help evaluate the children's needs.

Junior high or high school children may be embarrassed to have Mom come to school, but appreciate the fact that you want to help them. You may want to inform their teachers with a phone call when they aren't around to avoid embarrassing them. Teachers at the higher grade levels are often role models for students, especially if they are involved in special groups like band, choir, sports, or plays. If those teachers know a parent is gone, they may use the opportunity to show support for the young person without even specifically talking about Dad being away from home.

Don't be afraid to let the adults in your teenagers' lives know that Dad is deployed. Your teenagers may be more open to talking to adults outside of the family than to Mom. That's one reason it's important to know the people your youth relate to. They are learning to grow away from you as parents and to make their own decisions, and you can help them go through that process by giving them the freedom to talk to responsible adult friends.

Let your older children make the decisions they are ready to make and maintain open communication with them without smothering them. Even though they may seem to be very mature, Mom should not turn to her sons to take the place of Dad during deployments.

Don't ask boys to "be the man of the house" while Dad's away, or girls to "fill in for Mom" while she's gone. They aren't ready for that kind of responsibility, but take those requests very seriously. Allow them to be the children or teenagers they are. They don't have responsibility for your family and are not ready for that kind of burden.

However, children *are* ready to help with chores and some of the family's daily responsibilities; but don't make them feel like keeping the family together through the separation depends on them. They may be ready to take on the responsibility for keeping the car tires inflated or caring for the lawn, but they are *not* ready to take on the responsibility for keeping Mom from feeling depressed or being her companion while Dad is gone. Be sure to assign household chores to children in a way that helps them understand that they are *contributing* to the family, but not *responsible* for the family.

In addition to heightening your sensitivity to your children during the separation, there are more tangible things you can do to help them. Consider the following tips:

RELATING TO DAD

- Give each child a picture of himself or herself with Daddy.
- Every morning say "Good Morning," and at night say "Good Night" to Dad's picture with your child. You may want to add "see you soon!"
- Encourage each child to write to Dad regularly. If it's hard for them to begin, The Write Connection Program has some excellent resources you may want to consider. (Refer to the "Resources for Families" listed after this section of this book for more information.)
- Help each child think of things to send with a letter to Dad— artwork, school papers, or maybe a copy of a book report or assignment they did well on or are particularly proud of. Take a picture of your children with any special school projects they may have to make or at programs they may have a part in.

Maybe they'd like to record a tape to send (if Dad has the equipment to play it on). They may want to send a puzzle message (a letter cut into parts to assemble in order to read it).

- You may want to suggest that your child make an adventure out of writing to Dad. Liz Harte, a third grade teacher at a Department of Defense (DOD) Dependent School in Germany, had her class send foot-tall paper dolls to deployed parents. The class named the dolls Flat Stanleys, taken from a book by Jeff Brown (published in 1963). They sent their Stanleys on a mission to have an adventure and come back with a report. One Stanley came back with a journal: "Master Sergeant Jose Fontanez sent [Stanley back to his son Marcus with] a journal with photos. . . . First he and Stanley ate lunch. Then they visited the watchtower and motor pool. Stanley was photographed helping one of the soldiers install a part on a vehicle."[5] Major Tom O'Donovan wrote a letter to his daughter Meghan to tell her that he and Stanley shared a *Meal, Ready to Eat*.[6] When Chief Warrant Officer 2 Samuel Johnson received Stanley from his daughter Latreace, he showed Stanley to his co-workers and then showed Stanley around his work area, telling him what his work was like.[7] The class project helped the children feel closer to their absent parents. You can use the same idea at home. Get imaginative and have fun with it.
- You may want to have your children help you collect newspaper articles that relate to Dad's deployment[8] and put them in a scrapbook.
- Suggest that your children write multiple-choice letters to Dad. They could write parts of sentences, along with three or four options of endings, and ask Dad to mark the ones that are correct. For example, they might write the following:

  Dear Dad,
  This week my (a) teacher, (b) mother, (c) sister, or, (d) brother, was (a) nice, (b) naughty, or, (c) beautiful. I saw her in (a) math class, (b) reading class, (c) the principal's office, or, (d) the mall. I've been (a) good, (b) doing my homework, or, (c) making the dog do my homework.
  Love, (a) Susie, (b) Jane, or, (c) Bob

On the back of the page, they would give the answers: *answers: a,c,d,b,a*

- Suggest that the children draw a maze puzzle showing Dad where he is, and the house as the destination, and only one path that leads home. Send it to Dad and see if he can find his way home.

- Children may want to make a silhouette drawing of themselves to send Dad. They could have someone trace their bodies on butcher paper while they stand against the wall or lay on the floor. Or, they may want to send Dad one traced arm, hand, head, foot, or leg. They can draw pictures or write messages on the silhouette drawing to show Dad how they've grown or what they like to do.

- Your child may want to write a letter to Dad in code. The child could draw up a code by assigning a different letter or symbol to each letter of the alphabet. For example, ^ L^TT B<O says *I MISS YOU*.

- Even if your children do not write Dad regularly, they need to hear some kind of message from Dad on a regular basis. Children need to know that Dad is thinking about them and still loves them.

- You may want to give your child a calendar that has some room to write a message on each date, and ask them to write one thing they did each day on the calendar. At the end of each week or month, they could send their page of the calendar to Dad to help him keep up with their activities.

- Give your children's teachers stamped envelopes so they can send samples of your children's work to their Dad and tell him about their progress.

- Keep family pictures that include your husband out where your children will see them often.

- Make a map that shows Dad's deployed location and your home, and draw a line to connect the two locations. Hang it in a place where your children will see it often. You may want to attach pictures of your family at home and Dad where he is.

- Give the children tangible ways to feel connected to Dad on their own, like suggesting that when they look at the stars, Dad is probably looking at them, too. When her husband was deployed, Joey Diaz told their children that Daddy was away working on an airplane. "Whenever we saw an airplane go by, we talked about Daddy being on the airplane. Just kept telling them he was working and that he'd be home as soon as he could."[9]
- You may want to give your children toys that have a connection to what Dad's doing. Playing with airplanes, tanks, battleships, submarines, GI Joe, or other military-related toys may make them feel closer to Dad.
- You may want to start a "Things to tell Daddy Jar." Family members can write notes that can be saved in a jar for his return or mailed to him periodically.
- If Dad recorded any bedtime stories, play them before the children go to bed if they are used to having a story read to them at night.
- You may want to synchronize the child's alarm and Dad's watch or alarm so both will ring at the same time every day, and both the children and their father will be reminded of the other when they know they are hearing the alarm at the same time.
- If you can, give your children a way to measure the time until Dad will come home, such as crossing off days on a calendar. To give this a positive spin, you may want to make a paper chain to decorate the house for the homecoming, adding one chain link every day. Then if Dad's time away is lengthened, you can make comments about what a nice, big chain you are making, and won't that be a great surprise for Dad? Some families may use chains to count down, taking a link off every day, but that can be disappointing if the deployment is of uncertain length or the time is subject to change. Not many deployments are predictable, so I'd suggest finding some activity (that does not depend on the amount of time you are told your husband will be gone when he leaves) to help children count the days until Dad's return that counts upward.

SUPPORT AND ENCOURAGEMENT

Your children will probably have times during the deployment that they especially miss Daddy. Admit to your children that sometimes while Daddy is away you get sad and miss him too. Tell them that when we feel that way we can help each other. Maybe we can write Dad a letter, sing songs together, tell each other jokes, draw pictures, say extra prayers for our family, or just tell each other we love each other. Ask your children what you can do to cheer them up if they feel sad about Dad's being away. Other ideas you might find helpful are:

- Look for ways to compliment your children.
- If the separation is due to war or the absent parent is in danger, be open to talk to the children about it. Some children worry that they will also be in danger. Be honest with them as you reassure them; don't give them false hope or tell them things that may not be true (such as that no one will be hurt or die).
- Don't feel like you must have answers to everything. It's OK to tell children you don't know. You can give them the message that you'll do all you can to help them and keep them safe even though you can't answer all of the questions they may have.
- If your children aren't talking about how they feel, ask, and encourage them to ask you questions. Be honest with them and try to answer their questions in ways they can understand. It may be a good idea to "encourage dramatic play, including trying on military clothing, sleeping on cots, or wearing camouflage makeup."[10]
- If there is a support group for children of deployed personnel available in your area, involve your children. They will both be helped and help other children as they talk about issues that matter to them at the meetings.
- Show them on a map or globe where Dad is.
- Find ways to say you love them that are meaningful to each child.
- Give plenty of hugs.

- Reassure your children, in a way they can understand, that you'll take care of them and they don't have to worry about you leaving them, too. They need to know that your family won't fall apart, even though Daddy is gone for a while. When single parents are absent, be sure the care-provider you've chosen will nurture an extended family-type bond with your children to provide that same sense of security for the children.

BEHAVIOR

- Regression in toilet training or thumb sucking may be a response to the separation.
- Children may cling to you, or to a favorite toy or blanket.
- They may become more aggressive or have trouble getting along with their friends.
- Children may complain of stomachaches or headaches when nothing seems to be wrong.
- Try to keep them on the same schedule and same daily routines. They might need extra cuddling, hugging, or time with you, but continue your regular sleep and discipline practices. Try not to give in to the temptation to let children sleep with you instead of in their own beds.
- Set and keep your regular boundaries and rules.
- Avoid telling your children that when their father comes home they will be punished—carry out the discipline when the behavior occurs.
- Expect your children to test your limits. Give them discipline that is appropriate without overreacting to their behavior.
- Remember to laugh with them.
- Listen to your children and be available to talk when they want to talk. Listen to their behavior and attitudes as well as what they say. Keep good eye contact. Acknowledge their feelings and reflect them back to the child without judging or interpreting the feelings. Keep your words to a minimum.

- Take time to read them a book or watch TV with them.
- Read your children books that will help them understand the separation and reassure them that they will be OK. Children can usually relate better to a story in a book than to spoken concepts.
- Make craft projects or science projects that illustrate the normal change in seasons (pumpkins, snowflakes, leaves, seeds). Noticing seasonal changes will help children understand the passing of time, and may help them understand when their Dad will come home.
- Don't make unrealistic promises to your children to try to make them feel better. If you make a promise to them, be sure you can keep it and don't forget about it, because they won't forget and will be waiting for you to do what you said you would.
- When you become frustrated or angry with them, choose your words carefully.
- Don't neglect going on family outings just because Dad is gone. Take your children to the zoo, on picnics, or to the mall—whatever fits your family's interests and ages. Keep an atmosphere of fun alive in your family.
- Give your children the opportunity to help solve some of the smaller household problems that come up. (Do you need to check the air in your car's tires? How do we change the furnace filters? How do we replace lost keys? Can we fix a flat tire on the bicycle?) If you made a *Family Deployment Guide* before Dad left, ask one of your children to find the reference to help with the problem.

BABIES BORN DURING DEPLOYMENT

Sometimes military members must be away from their wives over holidays and important family events. The birth of a child may not wait for Dad's return, and he may have mixed feelings about that. His pride about the new child may be colored by apprehension about the responsibilities he faces, guilt or anger about not being at his wife's side for the birth, and concern that his wife and child are safe and well cared for.

While Dad is sorting through his feelings and wondering what the baby looks like and how he or she acts, Mom has her own conglomeration of responses to the birth. She may be feeling fulfilled and excited, enjoying the special bond with the new child. She may be feeling totally exhausted and overwhelmed with the responsibility of caring for the baby alone, especially if there are other children she has to take care of at the same time. Some new mothers experience the blues or even depression after a baby's birth.

Technology is now available to give some Dads that are away from home a chance to share a moment with their wives and new babies. Dalton Mills was on the aircraft carrier Enterprise in the Persian Gulf when his wife gave birth to their daughter in Chesapeake, Virginia. He was able to see his new baby through a video linkup between his ship and the Navy hospital in the States. "'I was fortunate to be one of the first,' Mills said. 'It's a big morale booster.' Not only for the guys at sea. Knowing that her husband has seen their new baby is making the rest of his deployment . . . easier for her to handle, Sherry Mills said. The mother of three no longer feels guilty that she alone has had the joy of seeing their daughter."[11]

However, the video linkup that the Mills' experienced is not available to everyone in the military. Most men who become fathers while on duty away from their families have to wait until they return home to see the baby. Both the husband and the wife want to be together to support one another and enjoy the new family member, but must find a way to do so from a distance. How is it possible to include the new father from a distance? Here are some ideas Mom may want to consider:

- Write Dad a letter to tell him about the birth experience.
- Write letters that describe the baby's looks, likes, dislikes, personalities, abilities, and growth.
- Send videotapes of the baby and mother, or audiocassettes of their voices, if Dad has the equipment to play tapes.

- Send pictures of the baby to Dad on a regular (maybe weekly) basis so he can see the baby change and grow.
- Send Dad a footprint or handprint of the baby, some hair, a shirt or bootie (so he can picture the size of the child), a hat, or anything that belongs to the baby that will help him feel connected.
- Write letters to Dad as if the baby were talking to Daddy.
- Keep a diary and baby book to share with Dad when he gets home.

1. Dahl, Barbara B., Edna J. Hunter, and Hamilton I. McCubbin, ed. *Families in the Military System.* (Beverly Hills, CA: Sage Publications, 1976), 301–309.
2. Doke, DeeDee. "Deployments among factors . . .", 16.
3. USAF. *Balancing Work & Life in the U. S. Air Force.* (Elkins Park, PA: Educational Publications, Inc., 1993), 52.
4. Cline, 213.
5. Arch, Tonja D. "Flat Stanleys bring kids tales from the front." *The Stars and Stripes,* European Edition, 14 June 1996: 3.
6. Ibid.
7. Ibid.
8. Seabolt, Amee. "Deployment Activities." *The Stars and Stripes,* European Edition, 27 January 1996: 17.
9. Zowie, Richard. "12th TRANS mechanic reflects on deployment," *Wingspread.* 10 January 2003; 4.
10. Seabolt, Amee. "Deployment Activities." *The Stars and Stripes,* European Edition, 27 January 1996: 17.
11. Doke, DeeDee. "Video Bridges the Miles for New Dad." *The Stars and Stripes,* 14 October 1996; 3.

· 7 ·

TAKING CARE OF YOURSELF
WHILE YOUR SPOUSE IS GONE

One squadron commander's wife told me that while her Special Forces husband was deployed with his unit, she was running all over the base to help the families under his command. One day she was called to her daughter's school, where the counselor told her that her daughter felt abandoned, because Dad was away and Mom was always gone to help someone. The daughter was having problems with the deployment, and Mom didn't even notice it because she was so busy helping everyone else. That was a wake-up call for her.

Others of us are more inclined to take care of our own needs, and those of our family first, and closely guard our time before we reach out. If you're like that, remember to think about what other families are going through, and when you're ready, reach out to them. Offer specific assistance you can see they could use, such as meals, babysitting, social outings like picnics, or inviting them to events they may not want to attend alone. Some friends invited me to go with them to the Art Auction on base while my husband was gone a few years ago, and I know I wouldn't have made the effort to get out if they hadn't invited me and offered to pick me up.

Caring for each other helps make sure our needs are met during deployments. Wives have spiritual needs, emotional needs, and physical needs that have to be met when their husbands are gone, and often they are so interrelated that meeting one need will help relieve another. Here are some ideas to help you get through separation:

Spiritual Needs

- See separation as an opportunity to grow rather than focusing only on the fact that your husband is deployed.
- Spend time daily in devotional reading, meditation, and prayer.
- Every day your husband is away, try to do something to improve yourself.
- Count your blessings regularly. Think about the good things in your life.
- Attend religious services and maintain your relationships with friends.

Emotional Needs

- Keep your husband's picture out where you'll see it often. Don't let him be out of sight and out of mind. If you feel overwhelmed, don't be afraid to ask for help, but don't compromise your marriage relationship by developing a close kinship and sharing personal problems with someone of the opposite sex. Spend time with opposite sex friends only in groups.
- Don't give in to the temptation to go live with parents or family members until your husband gets home. One wife said, "My first reaction was, 'Oh my God, how will I cope? What will I do for six months? I'll pack up and go home.' Then, I thought about it and decided to stick it out since my home is here now. I'm glad I did."[1] Try to think of wherever you live as your home instead of where your relatives are, and reassure yourself that you can live at home for a while without your husband.

Myrna Borling went to stay with relatives when her husband went to Vietnam in 1965. She said, "It was a wrong decision. I didn't have the support of the military community because I wasn't there, and there was no support from the civilians."[2] It is especially significant that Myrna said this after her husband's plane was shot down and he spent six and one-half years as a POW while she was in the civilian community with their relatives.

Civilians may ask why you are there without your husband and comment that they could never live like you do. In a civilian community, you also may not be near military health care, commissary, or other military family activities. Why put yourself in that awkward position when you could be in a community that understands your lifestyle and has benefits for your use?

> **What support do wives recognize as available to them during deployment?**
>
> 94% of wives said there was someone they could contact who would listen to them.
>
> 88% said there was someone they could go to for advice.
>
> 86% said there was someone they could have fun with.
>
> 85% said there was someone who gave them emotional support.
>
> 83% said there was someone they could get information from.
>
> 80% said there was someone they could go to if they needed transportation.
>
> 61% said they had someone they could call to take care of their children if there was an emergency.
>
> [Alder, Amy B., Ph.D., and Paul T. Bartone, Ph.D., and Mark A. Vaitkus, Ph.D. *USAMRU-E Technical Report 95-1: Family Stress and Adaptation During a U. S. Army Europe Peacekeeping Deployment.* U. S. Army Medical Research Unit-Europe. April 1995: 21–24]

- Don't turn to drugs, alcohol, smoking, or junk food when you feel down. Try to think of things to do that will make you laugh or lift your spirits instead. Maybe it would help to rent comedy videos or DVDs and have a friend over to watch them with you.
- Think about your body's cycles. Can you predict times when you might expect to feel moody, down, or tired? If you realize when those times are and expect them, it will be easier to separate them from your feelings of loneliness because of your husband's absence and to get through them without becoming depressed.
- Think about the good times you've shared with your husband and plan for more.
- From the first day of your separation, know where to go for help if you begin to feel overwhelmed. Then if the time comes that you feel the need to search out counsel, you will have phone numbers and names ready and it won't be as difficult for you.
- Some deployments are more stressful than others; don't compare yourself to other people. It's OK to feel like you don't understand everything. You don't have to be strong all of the time. Admit you have emotional needs without dwelling on your problems. The more you think about problems, the larger they will seem.
- Tell yourself you're doing a good job of maintaining the home by yourself once in a while. You probably are!
- Brainstorm ideas for leave time when your husband gets home.
- Think about long-term goals for your family. What do you want out of life? Share your ideas with your husband in a letter.
- Be flexible! See the unexpected and uncontrollable parts of life as adventures you can get through, even if they make you feel like you're finding your way through a maze.
- Initiate relationships with spouses of other deployed service members instead of waiting for someone to come to you. They are going through the same feelings and experiences that you are. Try to get together with them regularly during the deployment.

- Attend spouse support activities offered at your military installation (or the one nearest you if your husband was not Active Duty before the deployment). Depend on the military support network around you.
- If there is no support group near you, try to start one. Whether you have a formal group or informal home gathering, you need the support and encouragement of others who understand what you're going through.
- Don't listen to gossip or rumors. If your husband is in a hostile or dangerous environment and the media is covering the action 24-hours a day, avoid the temptation to stay glued to your TV. Listen to enough news to know what is happening and then turn it off. If you watch too much coverage, you will find more reasons to fear and worry. *Depend on your husband's chain of command or the support groups at your installation to receive information about your husband's situation, not the TV.*
- Remember that separations are often extended, so don't expect your husband's original return date to be reliable. Your husband wants to come home as soon as possible but has no control over that. Prepare yourself for the longest time period you think the separation could last, then expect the worst and hope for the best. Break the time up into manageable sections: get through one day or week or month at a time before you look ahead to the next day, week, or month. Find meaning in each day.
- If you begin to feel resentment that your husband is gone and you are left to handle everything, try to imagine how he feels about being away from the family. Knowing he also feels the pain of separation can help you not blame him for it. *Remember that you have the comfort and familiar atmosphere of home to enjoy. He doesn't.*
- Keep a journal. On days that are especially difficult, you may find encouragement as you look at earlier entries. The journal will also be a great record of what happened for your husband to read when he gets home.

- Do fun things with your children. Maybe you'd like to make a "treat ourselves to fun jar." Put ideas for fun things to do with the children on paper, and when you or your children need a lift or want to do something special, draw a paper out of the jar and do what it suggests. Children can help with ideas. Include each person's ideas and interests in the jar, and feel free to add to it as you think of things to do.
- Keep busy. Instead of thinking about what you and your husband are missing because of the separation, find a goal you can pursue that would be hard to accomplish if he was at home. Some ideas include: go back to school, get a part-time job, become more computer literate, do volunteer work, lose weight, begin a regular exercise program, grow a garden, clean out the closets, do a special craft or sewing project, learn to make picture frames, learn a foreign language, paint, or learn to play an instrument. If you smoke, surprise your husband and quit!
- You may enjoy having the company of a pet. (If you didn't have a pet before the separation, be sure that your husband won't object to an addition to the household.)

PHYSICAL NEEDS

- Eat right. (Here's your chance to eat the meals your husband doesn't like!)
- Get enough rest.
- Exercise regularly.
- Maintain your sense of humor.
- You can relax your housekeeping standards. Pamper yourself once in a while. Give yourself private time as often as you need it.
- If you have a question about military benefits or need a repair made, don't ask a neighbor that you think had a similar need. Go directly to the office or serviceperson who can help you. Don't be afraid to ask for clarification if you aren't sure you

understand what they say. If you need to, use your husband's chain of command to get help.

- If you need to go to any military or government office, call first to ask what documents you will need to accomplish your errand.
- Keep doors locked, even when you're at home. Use light and radio timers. Don't overreact and become housebound or fearful; just use common sense.
- Don't tell strangers your husband is gone. If telephone callers you don't know ask to speak to him, take a message and tell them you'll be sure he gets it. Tell babysitters how you want them to answer calls that may come for your husband when you are away.
- Don't talk about your husband's absence in public where strangers will hear you.
- Don't go out at night alone. When you are driving, always keep your car doors locked.
- Never let your car get below a quarter of tank of gas.
- Yellow ribbons and similar decorations advertise that someone is away unless the whole neighborhood decorates the same way. Wait until the day he returns to put out the yellow ribbon to welcome your husband home.
- Depend on your *Family Deployment Guide* to help you run your household. If your family didn't prepare one before the deployment, you can start making one now. Your husband will probably be proud of your effort.
- Give yourself realistic goals and schedules. Allow yourself time to relax without guilt.
- If you take a trip or leave home for any length of time, be sure your husband's commander knows how to reach you and where you are. Then if there's any information you need or an emergency that takes place, there will be no delay or problem locating you.

CHILDREN

- Make time to get out without your children. Spend time with positive, enthusiastic people. If you can't afford or find babysitters, ask a friend if she would be interested in trading babysitting with you.
- If you are a wife who works full time outside of the home, you may need to cut back on some of your other activities in order to have time to take care of your family without your husband's help. Your children may already feel the loss of their father, and if you are too busy to notice their feelings or spend time with them, they may feel like they've lost *both* of their parents. For their stability and security and for your own peace of mind, think about whether you should give up some of your outside-of-the-home involvements while your husband is gone.
- Be aware of how you respond to your children while your husband is gone. It is easy to overreact to their childish behavior and mistakes they make.

There are lots of things you can do to help yourself get through family separation. If you avoid the temptation to withdraw from others, you'll see that families and friends in the military community will gather together to care for each other during the hard times. The military emphasizes morale and quality of life issues more than they have in the past. This emphasis includes programs to help families during separation; anyone who looks for help or information should be able to find it.

1. Bartone, Paul T. *U. S. Army Families in USAREUR: Coping With Separation: Deployment Experiences of Army Spouses In Their Own Words.* U. S. Army Medical Research Unit-Europe: 3.
2. Interview with author, 16 September, 1999.

· 8 ·

OPSEC/COMSEC

We all know that for the military mission to succeed there has to be a certain amount of classified information. In military terms, OPSEC is Operations Security, and COMSEC is Communications Security. Do OPSEC and COMSEC affect military families? COMSEC definitely affected me when my husband was deployed to a classified location!

Soon after Ren left, I asked our Wing Chaplain for a list of other spouses whose husbands were gone, so I could connect with them. Because of privacy issues and COMSEC, he wouldn't share that list with me. He advised me to come to the support meeting, and I'd be able to meet other spouses there. I didn't mean to ask him to compromise information, but naively, and out of curiosity, asked him for information he couldn't give me. When I attended the meetings, I did meet other spouses, and we got together to do things after that.

From my perspective as a military wife, COMSEC can be thought of from an individual point of view as well as a social one. What I mean by an individual point of view is illustrated by my personal experience when my husband told me he was going to a classified location, and also when he called to give me his address. I had to resist the urge to ask questions that he couldn't answer, and that wasn't always easy. One thing that helped me refrain from asking him questions was knowing that his safety could be compromised. That meant I couldn't ask him questions, but also that I shouldn't expect him to tell me, even in confidence, where he was. I didn't have a *need to know*. So, to exercise good COMSEC, I didn't talk about it.

The social view of COMSEC means that I didn't talk about location even with spouses whose husbands were at the same location as mine. If we had talked about where they were, or what type of aircraft there were at their locations, or even information as simple as what specific jobs some of our husbands did, that could have put them in danger. The more people know, the greater the possibility that they will talk about what they know in public: on telephones, in restaurants, at their churches, while they're shopping, or at places like night clubs, Officer's and Enlisted Clubs.

When we were stationed overseas, the Armed Forces TV Network had public service videos in place of state-side advertising. I remember one of the videos in Okinawa that showed two people talking in a restaurant, and a spy listening to them. The spy was dressed in a trench-coat, hat and gloves, writing on a note pad as he listened, to give the visual image of the danger, and we laughed at that. But the message was real and we need to remember it. Spies and terrorists may not look any different than the person who sits at the next table at the restaurant you go to, or shops next to you in the store. Little bits of information, that may not even be classified, can help people with bad intentions fill out the picture. So, don't talk about details of your military life that don't need to be shared.

If you hear someone else talking, remind them that it's better not to talk about what our spouses do or where they are. It's our responsibility to remind each other that when we talk to one person, it's easier to talk to another later, so to prevent sharing potentially sensitive information, we shouldn't talk at all. It's better not to say anything to anyone. That includes your children. Children don't understand what they should or shouldn't talk about, so don't give them information that they shouldn't spread in public.

Talking publicly about your husband's absence could also potentially put *you* at risk. Whether it's politically correct to say so or not, women alone make good targets. That's one reason I recommend that you don't hang a yellow ribbon in your window unless everyone else on your street does. Don't advertise that you're alone.

If you absolutely *can't* resist talking to someone, talk with your chaplain. Chaplains are the only military members with complete confidentiality, and will not share what you talk with them about.

However, COMSEC doesn't mean there is no communication. When my husband was deployed to a classified location, on a couple of occasions I received phone calls from air crew members from our base who told me they were going to go to my husband's location, and if I had anything I'd like them to bring to Ren, they'd take it for me. Without divulging any secrets, they gave me support and consideration by their availability and willingness to provide a link between my husband and me.

There were other wives whose husbands were deployed with mine, but when we visited with each other, we didn't talk about where they were. They were all away working for a common mission, and we were all at home having similar experiences. Instead of exercising our curiosity about things we can't know, let's be proud of our military spouses and support them.

· 9 ·

SUPPORT GROUPS

Support Groups can take a variety of forms of organization, from informational meetings with question and answer time to group therapeutic discussions. Don't be afraid to go to meetings to see what specific groups offer. Most groups welcome visitors and you don't have to go back every time they meet if you don't want to. Deployment support groups on military installations are usually informal and informational. Whether they are organized by the Family Service Centers, the chapel, or military units, their purpose is the same: to make life better for the families of deployed personnel.

Families of deployed personnel need to think about what encourages and comforts them when they feel overwhelmed. During deployments, they will need encouragement and support. They can help create it.

When my husband was deployed, there was a formal Dining Out to celebrate the Air Force's Birthday; since I lived on base, I could see everyone in their mess dress uniforms and formal dresses leaving for the party. The wives of other deployed service members in one squadron on our base had adopted me into their group, and the night of the Dining Out, we got dressed up and went to a nice restaurant for our own celebration. We gathered all of the children at one house, where the teenagers babysat the younger children. About twelve wives had a nice evening out, and about twenty-five kids had a pizza party with balloons and games. We ended the evening watching a video some of the husbands had sent, showing their tent city and deployed location. Instead of feeling left out, we all felt encouraged.

COMMAND SUPPORT

When my husband was deployed, our base had weekly support meetings that were held at the base chapel. At every meeting, there were representatives from the Post Office, legal office, Red Cross, Family Services, chapel, public affairs, and Base Exchange, along with the Base Commander and the Wing Commander. They gave us information about mail flow, how to deal with people who were reluctant to accept our Powers of Attorney, what services were available to our husbands, and much more.

When the media asked wives for interviews, the requests came through Public Affairs to protect our privacy. When a professional sports team in our area offered free tickets to families of deployed personnel, I heard about it (and got the information I needed to

What are wives' biggest frustrations during deployment?
Wives in the Army study said their biggest frustrations were wondering what will happen to their husbands' units, not knowing when their husbands would be back, lack of sufficient information, lack of a good Family Support Group, divorce, no information at all, being jerked back and forth between delays and orders that the unit was leaving, no alternation of troops, childcare, unsuccessful Family Support Group meetings, no Family Support, and no support from the chain of command.

[Alder, Bartone, and Viatkus, 19.]

get tickets) at the support meeting. Other businesses in the area donated T-shirts and food to deployed families, and we received information about that at the meetings, too. We were even treated to meals after a couple of the meetings.

The commanders helped us sort through rumors during question and answer sessions every week and told us what they knew was factual or exaggerated in the news. One wife had a problem with her quarters and needed help getting the housing office to take care of it, and the Base Commander offered to talk to housing. Another wife was having problems with her bank because their checking account was new and didn't have her name on it when it was opened, and the lawyer from the Base Legal Office offered to go to the bank with her to try to straighten out the problem.

UNIT SUPPORT GROUPS

Many military units also organize support groups for families of those who are deployed. Unit commanders and other leaders usually know the military members in their units personally, and also know their families. When someone from a unit is deployed, there is often a network of familiar people ready to help the families that are left behind. They may help by holding group meetings, through personal contacts, or there may be a unit newsletter or telephone information chain to keep families informed.

When my husband was deployed, he was deployed individually, not with a unit. There was a squadron at our base that had a number of people deployed to a different location than my husband, and in the spirit of military camaraderie, that squadron adopted me during the time my husband was deployed. The wives of those in the squadron who were deployed got together for dinner, shopping, and picnics with their children, and included me.

One Saturday the men of the squadron held a car-care day for the spouses of those who were gone. We all brought our cars over to the auto hobby shop, and while we ate the pizza they provided and their families played with our children, they changed our oil and filters, checked hoses, checked tires, etc. I was thankful for that, because their examination of our car revealed that I had a bad spot in one of my tires and it needed to be replaced. So they were kind enough to tell me where to get one and saved me a blowout. I appreciated their sensitivity to include me in their unit during that time.

Support in the Military Community

Unit support often extends beyond the confines of the unit sponsoring the activity, although the attention naturally is focused on unit needs. Unit commanders and leaders provide encourage-ment to families just by showing interest in how they are doing during the separa-tion and listening carefully to pick up on needs that they may be able to help meet. When personnel under his command are deployed, one commander writes notes to the parents of his young troops to tell them that he knows they probably feel a bit anxious about the son or daughter, but as the com-mander he will be sure they are doing well. He also offers his phone number and that of his First Sergeant, encour-aging the parents to call if

How do wives cope with problems when their hus-bands are deployed?
To cope with their most im-portant problems, 93% of wives said they take one day at a time, 90% said they would talk with their hus-bands, 86% would try to find more information, 84% would talk with a friend, and 83% said they would write a letter to their husbands.

[Alder, Bartone, and Vaitkus, 19.]

they have concerns or need assistance. In addition to caring com-manders, your installation may have ombudsman or key volun-teers who are sensitive to the needs of families and ready to help when there is a need.

There are countless examples of how spouses and families have been supported that could be listed. My husband told me that the morale of troops who knew their wives or families were attending support groups was better than the morale of those whose wives were not. Troops who knew their families had support back home didn't worry as much about their families, so they were happier and more able to concentrate on their mission. For me, the spouse support meetings were both a connection to the military while my husband was gone and a source of encouragement to help me through the separation. My relatives could not have given me the same kind of support and encouragement.

Most Active Duty military families don't live near their relatives, so they can't look to them for support. Even those with relatives near by may find that relatives don't understand the military lifestyle and can't identify with their unique needs, even though they may sincerely love them and try to understand. If your relatives haven't lived the military lifestyle, they're limited in their ability to help meet your needs. The military is different from the civilian culture around it and has a reputation for caring for its own. ". . . the military subculture, with its interpersonal relationships and its tradition of mutual help, plays a potentially significant and primary role in helping families cope with the stress of military separation."[1] Becoming involved in the military network and making use of its resources will be more satisfying and helpful to most military spouses and families than going back home to their relatives.

SUPPORT FOR RESERVE AND GUARD FAMILIES

The Reserve and Guard components have family support groups available as the need arises. Their families can also take part in support groups offered on Active Duty installations.

However, Reserve and Guard families may not live near enough to an installation to benefit from the support the military community provides. Often Reserve and Guard members drive a distance to their drill areas, so their families are not close to the unit. They may not have an opportunity to meet or form friendships with families of those that serve with their husbands. These Reserve and Guard families may receive the support they need during mobilizations and deployments from their extended families and their churches. The relationships they have in their civilian communities provide a sense of continuity and stability that helps them endure the family separation.

There are some needs that the civilian community cannot meet. Although Reserve and Guard families may not be near enough to an Active Duty installation or local unit to use many of their military benefits, they have access to some benefits wherever they live. One such benefit may be CHAMPUS or TRICARE. In order to use the medical benefits, Reserve and Guard families may need to call someone in the military system for help. Active Duty families also have to know who to call when they need help. The military tries to meet the needs of families of every component, but individual service members can help by telling their families how to use their benefits and giving them the names and phone numbers of military personnel who can answer questions after they deploy.

WHY SUPPORT GROUPS ARE IMPORTANT/HOW TO HELP EACH OTHER

An Army study showed that many wives were either reluctant to use the resources the military offered or did not know about them. These wives were mailed information about the resources that were available before their husbands were deployed. Some wives didn't know whether they should use the military resources because they were afraid it would reflect negatively on their husband's careers. The sad result was that the support and help the military offered was underused.[2] The same study showed that wives who thought the Army provided enough support for them had less depression than wives who were dissatisfied, verifying that Army support is important to family adjustment to separations.[3] This is true for any branch or component of the military. Knowing that someone cares and is there when you need help enables you to remain more calm and confident when you are separated from your spouse.

Spouses do not go to military support meetings to receive charity or pity. Attending a military spouse support group one time

What do wives see as their biggest problems when their husbands are deployed?
The majority (76.7%) said missing their husband's companionship was the most difficult problem they had to cope with. After that they cited loneliness, having to make decisions alone, decrease in their social life, concern for their health, and guilt about taking the role of leadership at home.

[Dahl, Hunter, and McCubbin, 119.]

will show you that it is a place for you to meet other families who are going through the same things you are. Support groups provide help as well as enable you to help others. There may be someone who has a problem larger than yours that you are able to help, or a need for volunteers may be presented that interests you. Others will share what helps them and you can do the same. The purpose is to help each other get through separations, and military organizations hold meetings because they want to help families survive in the best way possible.

Whether your deployment is due to a war, peacekeeping or humanitarian mission, or other duty, the separation will result in some form of fear or anxiety. Some issues that cause concern are the following: not knowing exactly where the service member is or whether he has arrived at the deployed site; wondering what danger the service member may face; media reports of fighting or unrest in the husband's location; not hearing from the husband for some time; not knowing how to contact him; communication from him that shows that he's afraid; uncertainty about the amount of time the husband will be gone; not knowing how to show the husband support; not knowing anything about his situation; uncertainty about managing the home over an extended time without the husband; concern about the health and welfare of family members in both locations; concern about the family's finances; and concern about the husband's reintegration into the family.[4] Whether family stress is caused by these or other concerns, it will wear down the ability to resist depression, irritability, or feelings of being overwhelmed.

> "The major source of stress was deployment; factors such as uncertainty about the length of deployment, missing one's spouse, difficulties in communication, concern about spouse's safety and living conditions produced considerable distress among the respondents." [Rosenberg, 37.]

Many families experience distress because of repeated changes of the departure time or because the departure interferes with family vacation plans or visits to relatives before the family member deploys. We had non-refundable airplane tickets that we had to try to get returned. If you find yourself in that situation, call the airline or travel agent. Tell them that unexpected military duty has changed your plans, and ask whether they can refund your ticket or give you a credit voucher for later travel if you send them a copy of your husband's orders or a letter from his commander on official letterhead. Most airlines are understanding and will accommodate your request.

In addition to feeling overwhelmed after the husband leaves, the family may have to deal with the disappointment of not being able to go on a family trip they looked forward to. To prevent these feelings from taking over, the family must find a means of strength to cope with the extra demands they face. "The more we treat people as unable to cope, the less able to cope they become. Family members need support, not smothering; they need to be reminded of their strengths, not their weaknesses; they need to be invited to do what they can for themselves, not to have others do more and more for them."[5]

If you've been through family separation before and you know someone who is going through one for the first time, find ways to help them help themselves. Toni Shamlee said, "With this being the first deployment for my husband and me, I acted out of anger and fear. . . . Just remember that for spouses who are going through this for the first time, understanding and support are needed."[6] Both spouses who are going through separation for the first time and those who have been through separations before need support when their families are affected by deployment. They can probably help and encourage each other.

If you've been through family separation before, invite someone to the spouse or family support meeting at your military installation and to church or community meetings that are meaningful to you. If you have not been separated from your spouse before, look for meetings that will help you learn more about how to get through deployment. Ask your chaplain or someone in your spouse's chain of command (for example, First Sergeant, Chief Petty Officer, unit commander, or ombudsman) if you don't know whether there are meetings on your installation. Many installations have family support meetings, and individual units often have small groups that meet in addition to the family meetings. Don't miss your opportunity to receive all of the information and encouragement these groups offer.

1. Dahl, Hunter, and McCubbin, 162.
2. Alder, Amy B., Ph.D., and Paul T. Bartone, Ph.D., and Mark A. Vaitkus, Ph.D. *USAMRU-E Technical Report 95-1: Family Stress and Adaptation During a U. S. Army Europe Peacekeeping Deployment.* U. S. Army Medical Research Unit-Europe. April 1995: 5.
3. Ibid.
4. Paap, 20–25.
5. Paap, 80.
6. Shamlee, Toni A. "Understanding Needed." *The Stars and Stripes,* European Edition, 5 February 1996: 12.

· 10 ·

The Role of Faith during Separation

Many people feel emptiness or gaps in their lives when their families are separated or are in uncertain circumstances. That empty feeling can be turned into something positive.

"In the first place nothing can fill the gap when we are away from those we love, and it would be wrong to try and find anything. We must simply hold out and win through . . . It is nonsense to say that God fills the gap: He does not fill it, but keeps it empty so that our communion with another may be kept alive, even at the cost of pain . . . Times of separation are not a total loss, nor are they completely unprofitable for our companionship . . . In spite of all the difficulties they bring, they can be a wonderful means of strengthening and deepening fellowship. . . We must commend our loved ones wholly and unreservedly to God and leave them in his hands, transforming our anxiety for them into prayers on their behalf." Dietrich Bonhoeffer, Tegel Prison, Berlin, Christmas Eve, 1944.[1]

The emptiness you feel when your husband is gone can become a reminder to pray for him. Viktor Frankl, Holocaust survivor and Swiss psychiatrist, maintains that one can face any crisis if the person grasps some meaning or purpose in it.[2] Many couples find meaning or purpose during times of separation by thinking more deeply about their spiritual lives, individually and on the family level.

Being separated from the ones they love may make people think about what life would be like if the spouse didn't come back, especially if the spouse is in harm's way. The complete lack of control over the situation produces feelings of anxiety. David Paap says that "The only practical escape from this vicious cycle of anxiety is a spiritual one: trust in God. . . . faith and trust differ from human optimism or self-confidence in that they are not the result of human effort or reliance upon anything within ourselves."[3] Paap is convinced that faith is the most important factor that determines how a family facing the crisis of deployment or war will deal with their members' fears.

People often turn to God during crisis. When traumatic events occur the media broadcasts public references to prayer and looking to God for help. Faith gives people the hope and courage they need to get through trials. When they feel like they have nowhere else to turn, God is there. The realization that you have no control over circumstances may draw you to God for the first time, or possibly back to God. "The power is in the Person to whom faith clings. . . . The great things that come about through crisis are not the result of 'great faith' but of faith, even a small and flickering faith, in the greatness of God's love and mercy in Jesus Christ."[4] It is the God your faith is in, not the greatness of your faith, which will get you through.

Each morning, whether you're separated from a family member or not, you may find it helpful to begin the day looking to God for guidance and strength for the day. The military lifestyle gives you unique opportunities to experience the peace and grace of God during hard times. Chaplain Stan Beach said, "When my situation can't be changed, I can work at learning and implementing productive responses that will honor the Lord."[5] Denise McColl said, "A good friend once told me, 'Pray as if everything depended on God; work as if everything depended on you!' Applying this concept works wonders during deployments!"[6] Sue

Roberts advises separated families to "not pray for an easy life; pray to be a strong person."[7]

Admiral Grady Jackson said, "In many ways I've never been closer spiritually to my family than when I've been away from them for extended periods, because those are the times I fully put them into the Lord's hands. When we move out in the job that the Lord has called us to do, He will take care of our families, especially if His call requires separation."[8]

Worry about the family back home is one of the greatest concerns military service members face, but many families find that sharing in letters how faith is active in their lives helps ease that concern. Finding things to thank God for helps keep attitudes positive. If you consider yourself to be a believer but do nothing special to nurture your faith, you may find that a daily personal devotional time will help keep you positive and spiritually strong.

Remember that God is with you anywhere you go, even in the most isolated place the military may send you. When you're away from your family, it's easy to feel like you aren't accountable to them; separation may offer temptations that would threaten your relationship with your spouse and that are hard to resist. Statistics tell us that many marriages break down during times of separation because of the temptation to be unfaithful. One Marine who recognized that danger and wanted to protect himself from temptation developed his own set of guidelines to follow whenever he is away from his wife. They include the following:

- Temptation is easier to resist when we are closer to God, so devote the time you would otherwise have with your family to deepening your relationship to God.
- Find others who share your faith for friendship and prayer.
- Guard your eyes. When pornography tempts you, consciously remind yourself to fill your mind with movies, books, and magazines that encourage Godly living.
- Consistently communicate with your wife.
- Always be accountable for your time during times of liberty. Don't go ashore alone, but go with someone you know will

help you avoid temptations. Avoid the appearance of evil. If people know you are a Christian, they will be silently watching to see whether you practice what you preach.
- Be alert. Realize that temptation can sneak up on you.[9]

These guidelines may be points you want to consider for yourself, or you may already have your own drawn up. The important issue is to face the fact that temptation and unfaithfulness will likely be present whether you are the deployed husband or the wife at home, and you can help yourself resist if you have a plan to stay committed to your spouse. Christians are not exempt from challenges to marriage and should assume that they, too, *will* be tempted.

God will not be overcome by the challenges or temptations we face, so if we turn to Him, we can feel safer, too. His representatives, the chaplains or ministers we look to for guidance, remind us that we don't have to be afraid, and they help us direct our attention to God.

When you feel overwhelmed, turn to the Lord Himself. As you cultivate your relationship with God and feel the encouragement of your chapel or place of worship, you will be more equipped to deal with separation. "I encourage you to lean on someone during this deployment. I have been going to the Darmstadt International Baptist Church, and during this time in my life when I could be feeling absolutely alone in the world, I have been overwhelmed with a sense of support and love from my church family."[10]

With the support of others and your sense of God's strength within, you will be able to identify with the apostle Paul when he said, "We are hard-pressed on every side, yet not crushed; we are perplexed, but not in despair; persecuted, but not forsaken; struck down, but not destroyed . . ."[11] In addition to the strength and help you draw from your personal faith, your chapel or place of worship may offer a support group for encouragement.

Military chaplains experience deployment and family separation too, and know what you're feeling. Who could be better equipped to help you through tough times? God and His representatives stand ready to meet your needs.

1. USAF Chaplain Service Institute, *Link,* 29.
2. Beach, "Enduring and Prospering in Your Military Calling," 5.
3. Paap, 29.
4. Ibid, 82.
5. Beach, Captain Stan J., Chaplain, U. S. Navy (Retired). "Praise the Lord Anyway." *Command* (Fall 1989) Vol. 38, No. 3: 3.
6. McColl, Denise. "Making the Most of Deployments: A Wife's Perspective." *Command,* (Fall 1989) Vol. 38, No. 3: 12.
7. Roberts, 45.
8. Jackson, Admiral Grady. "President's Letter." *Command* (Fall 1989) Vol. 38, No. 3: 1.
9. Heinle, Major D. R., U. S. Marine Corps. "Marital Fidelity in Far-Away Places," in *Deployed, Not Disconnected: Hope and Help for Husbands and Wives Facing Separations Due to Military Assignments,* ed. by Don and Karen Martin. (Englewood, CO: OCF Books, 1991), 100–101.
10. Modawell, Jelaine. "Look to God." *The Stars and Stripes,* European Edition, 26 January 1996: 20.
11. *The Holy Bible,* The New King James Version, II Corinthians 4:8,9.

· 11 ·
RESOURCES TO HELP YOU DURING DEPLOYMENT

RESOURCES FOR DEPLOYING PERSONNEL

- **Web sites operated by the National Institute for Building Long Distance Relationships**
  All of these web sites have great links, ideas, and information.

  www.daads.com
  Dads at a Distance—helps fathers who are away from their children maintain and strengthen their relationships during their absence.

  www.momsovermiles.com
  Moms Over Miles—helps mothers who have to be away to maintain and strengthen the relationships they have with their children while they're gone.

  www.longdistancecouples.com
  Long Distance Couples—helps couples maintain relationships with each other when they're separated.

www.longdistancegrandparenting.com
Grandparenting from a Distance.

- *101 Ways to Be A Long-Distance Super Dad . . . or Mom, Too!*
  by George Newman
  Available from:
    Blossom Valley Press
    5141 E. Woodgate
    P.O. Box 13378
    Tucson, AZ 85732-3378
    phone: (520) 325-1224

- *Deployment Devotions*
  Available from:
    Resource Division of the USAF Chaplain Service Institute
    CPD/HCX
    525 Chennault Circle
    Maxwell AFB, AL 36112

- *A Special Prayer Service in Support of Deploying Forces and Families*
  Prayers, hymns, and Scripture selections specifically for deployed forces, their families, and our nation.
  Available from:
    Creative Communications for the Parish
    1564 Fencorp Drive
    Fenton, MO 63026
    (800) 325-9414
    www.creativecommunications.com

RESOURCES FOR FAMILIES

- *The Business Traveling Parent*
  How to Stay Close to your Kids When You're Far Away

by Dan Verdick
Mr. Verdick includes activities to do with your children before you leave, while you're gone, and when you get back home. He also gives resources to expand on some of his ideas.
Published by: Robins Lane Press
Beltsville, MD
www.robinslane.com
Available at bookstores. If the bookstore near you does not have it, ask them to order it.

- *Command*
  Issue devoted to deployment: Fall 1989 issue, Volume 38, No. 3
  Available from:
  Officer's Christian Fellowship
  3784 South Inca
  Englewood, CO 80110
  e-mail: ocfdenver@ocfhq.org

- *Heroes at Home: Help & Hope for America's Military Families*
  by Ellie Kay

- *Service Separations: A Wife's Perspective*
  by Beverly Moritz
  Available from:
  Focus on the Family
  8605 Explorer Drive
  Colorado Springs, CO 80995
  (800) 232-6459
  www.family.org
  or:
  Officer's Christian Fellowship
  3784 South Inca
  Englewood, CO 80110
  e-mail: ocfdenver@ocfhq.org
  www.gospelcom.net/ocf

- *Memories of Me,* for children ages 4–12
  WriteBack Mail
  The letter-writing kits include stationery, envelopes, calendars, and stickers, and are available in Standard or Military versions. They also offer a letter-writing idea book and craft projects. These resources may be available at your Family Support Center, or you can contact the publisher:

  The Write Connection Co.
  Letter Writing Program
  P. O. Box 293
  Lake Forest, CA 92630
  (714) 581-3283
  (800) 334-3143
  Fax (714) 859-0405

- **Published by Channing L. Bete Co.:**
  About Deployment
  Meeting the Challenges of Deployment
  Until Your Parent Comes Home Again; a coloring and
      activities book about deployment
  Your Parent is Coming Home; a coloring and activities book
  Let's Talk About Reunion; an information and activities book
  Let's Talk About Deployment; an information and activities
      book
  Deployment Days; a coloring calendar for military families
  What You Should Know About Stress and Your Child
  Family Support Groups
  Make the Most of Family Support Groups
  Military Families Are Special; a coloring and activities book
  Living in a Military Family
  Military Family Life
  MISSION: READINESS: A Personal and Family Guide
  Available from your Family Support Center, your chaplain or
  the publisher:
      Scriptographic Booklets
      Channing L. Bete Co. Inc.

200 State Road
South Deerfield, MA 01373-0200
(800) 477-4776
e-mail: custsvcs@channing-bete.com
www.channing-bete.com

- **Published by The Bureau For At-Risk Youth:**
  Coloring Book: *I'll Miss You*
  Titles in the Family Forum Library—Military Edition:
  How to Be a Successful Young Military Family
  Parenting Your Young Children in the Military
  Anger Management and Conflict Resolution in the Military
  Deployment and Reunion: Challenges and Opportunities
  Successfully Parenting Your Adolescent in the Military
  Effective Child Discipline for Successful Military Families
  School and the Military Family
  The Military Lifestyle and Children
  Moving and the Military Family
  Loss and Change in the Military Family
  Family Readiness
  Stress and the Military Family
  Communication Skills for the Military Family
  Titles from the For Parents Only Series:
  Dealing With Your Child's Feelings
  Encouraging a Positive Attitude
  Teaching Your Child the Value of Friendship
  Teaching Your Child to Appreciate Diversity
  Building Positive Parent/Child Communication
  Teaching Your Child to Make Smart Choices
  Getting Along Better With Your Child
  Keeping Your Child Drug-Free
  Building Your Child's Self-Esteem
  Teaching Conflict Resolution Skills
  Teaching Your Child Responsibility
  Motivating Your Child to Success

Available from your Family Support Center, your chaplain, or the publisher:
The Bureau For At-Risk Youth
135 Dupont Street
P.O. Box 760
Plainview, NY 11803-0760
(800) 99-YOUTH
e-mail: info@at-risk.com
www.at-risk.com

- **Published by Abbey Press:**
  When You Miss Someone Deeply, During a Time Apart
  Taking Time for Yourself When You're Feeling Stress
  Letting Faith Help You Handle Stress
  Doing Your Best as a Single Parent
These titles are Care Notes, published by Abbey Press. Ask your chaplain if these titles are available at your chapel or if your chapel can provide them.

- *Today's Military Wife: Meeting the Challenges of Service Life*
  by Lydia Sloan Cline
  Available at bookstores; published by: Stackpole Books.

- **Web sites operated by the National Institute for Building Long Distance Relationships**
  All of these web sites have great links, ideas, and information.

  www.daads.com
  Dads at a Distance—helps fathers who are away from their children maintain and strengthen their relationships during their absence.

  www.momsovermiles.com
  Moms Over Miles—helps mothers who have to be away to maintain and strengthen the relationships they have with their children while they're gone.

www.longdistancecouples.com
Long Distance Couples—helps couples maintain relationships with each other when they're separated.

www.longdistancegrandparenting.com
Grandparenting from a Distance.

- *Handbook for Military Families*
Supplement to *Army Times, Navy Times,* and *Air Force Times,* in April (updated yearly)
Available by subscription, at military exchanges, and in many libraries.

NAVY RESOURCES

- *Daddy's Days Away*
A deployment activity book for parents and children.

Navy Programs and Workshops

- **Keeping in Touch**
The CO (usually of a ship) writes a familygram newsletter to keep family and friends informed about the command. The ombudsman is available to mediate between the military and families. An informal telephone tree consisting of command family members passes on information of interest to everyone in the command, such as changes to a ship's schedule.

- **"Gator-Aid" for Mid-Deployment**
Family members are enabled to cope with mid-deployment blues and focus on plans for the homecoming through discussion and activities.

RESOURCES FOR MILITARY CHAPEL OR CIVILIAN CHURCH CONGREGATIONS

- *The Other War*
  A 20-minute videotape and discussion guide with an extensive resource list, for use in ministering to those afflicted by war.
  Available from:
  > Concordia Publishing House
  > (800) 325-3040
  > www.cph.org

- *A Special Prayer Service in Support of Deploying Forces and Families*
  Prayers, hymns, and scripture selections specifically for deployed forces, their families, and our nation.
  Available from:
  > Creative Communications for the Parish
  > 1564 Fencorp Drive
  > Fenton, MO 63026
  > (800) 325-9414
  > www.creativecommunications.com

III

REUNION

· 1 ·

FINALLY, IT'S OUR TURN!

We were still having spouse support meetings every week, but fewer and fewer wives came. Many of my friends stopped coming for the second time. They were wives of tanker crews, and their husbands deployed on 45-day or 90-day rotations, since the planes had to come back home to be serviced that often. I was the one consistent attendee who had been there through the whole thing.

When Ren left, his orders said he would be deployed for 90 days. Lots of orders said that. When they began to deploy people in August they could only guess how long it would be. When I said goodbye to Ren, something inside told me he wouldn't be home for Christmas. I was right.

At the support meetings, they announced when planes were coming in with people returning from the Gulf so that everyone who could and wanted to would be there to welcome them home. There was a chart in the front of the room that held yellow ribbons, each bearing the name of someone who had been deployed and returned. Yellow ribbons were everywhere but, so far, none had Ren's name written on them. It became almost a ritual for someone to come up to me and say, "It should have been your turn before mine. Your husband has been gone longer than anyone on our base." That didn't make the waiting any easier.

On the 215th day after Ren left, it was finally my turn. He flew into the commercial airport. I wanted to have a quiet, private reunion with Ren and Dan, but there were a lot of people from the base who wanted to welcome him home, too, so our private family time would have to wait.

I was overwhelmed by the number of people at the airport to welcome him home! There were video cameras and people everywhere. I felt conspicuous, on exhibition. When he came through the security checkpoint at the airport, he was surprised to see the people there to greet him. We embraced awkwardly, conscious of the throng surrounding us waiting to shake his hand, the video camera capturing every move we made.

I tried to hurry him through the handshakes. He said "hello" to each one, not wanting to leave anyone unacknowledged for coming to greet him.

"Get him out of here," the commander told me.

I tried, but he didn't want to hurt anyone's feelings by hurrying away too quickly. I had to remind myself not to feel hurt that he felt that way. After 215 days apart, I could wait a few more minutes.

We finally got in the car but hardly knew where to start, except to agree that it sure was good to be back together. That was a good place to start. Yes, start. It may have been the end of the deployment, but we had to begin life together again after a 215-day separation.

· 2 ·

BACK HOME, SWEET HOME

You've just heard when the family separation will end, and are happy to think about being a complete family again. Those at home are busy making preparations for the homecoming, while the deployed husband envisions home as he left it. Family members at both locations have to prepare to reunite and realize that things will be different than they were before, or the relief of being together will soon fade into discontent.

CHANGE IS INEVITABLE

Every member of the family has probably changed during the separation. Changes can be as obvious as physical growth of the children or the birth of a new baby, a spouse's new job, weight loss or gain, or a new hairstyle. Changes may be less definable, such as greater independence, feelings of anger about the separation, uncertainty about whether the husband will still feel the same way about the family, fear about the changes that have occurred within each family member and how those changes will affect the family. The amount of change that takes place in the family depends on the individual family and the length of the separation.

Longer separations typically cause more emotional pain and adjustment, and also produce the need for more understanding and patience when the family is reunited. The family at home may have developed a new routine or taken on extra activities to help them deal with the husband and father's absence. Everyone in the family has to be sensitive as they decide together whether they'll continue the new pattern when he gets back, try to go back to the way they did things before the deployment, or form a different, revised version of family life.

For example, children grow and respond to different kinds of discipline as they gain understanding. Maybe when Dad left the child responded to a slap on the hand, but while Dad was gone the child progressed to the point where he responds better to being sent to his room to think about what he did, followed with a parent-child discussion about the proper behavior. Little children may not recognize Dad when he gets home or may feel afraid of him at first.

These and other differences can add stress to the joy of being reunited as a family. The "Eastern Virginia Medical Association states that reunion and homecoming are more stressful than the initial pre-deployment and deployment phase."[1] Richard D. Thompson acknowledges that most people know that reuniting the family is another beginning rather than end and that letters cannot substitute for family experiences in life. He says that families should renew their relationships by discovering "what changes have occurred in each person,"[2] rather than concentrating on the tension of the change.

Change can be negative or positive. Change often makes us feel afraid, or as if we've lost something comfortable. We can choose not to dwell on the fear or loss involved in change, and even though the process of change often hurts, we can learn to see the growth and benefits that result from change. Of course, this process takes time.

If the wife has been attending individual or family support groups during the husband's absence, it will probably be helpful to continue attending those meetings for at least a few weeks after he

returns. Attending the meetings will give the family a sense of continuity as they work through the process of reuniting the family, as
well as show the husband how the family received support and
encouragement when he was gone. Many returning husbands are
encouraged to see for themselves the support their families had
while they were gone, and they're proud that their families participated in a support group. Attending the group meetings as a complete family can help the family find a starting point to talk about
what happened during the separation and understand each other's
needs and feelings related to the deployment.

1. Thompson, Richard D. "Homecoming: A Period of Adjustment." *Military
    Chaplains' Review,* Transitions (Winter 1991): 29.
2. Ibid, 21.

· 3 ·

PREPARING YOUR FAMILY
FOR REUNION

Each member of the family has needs resulting from the separation, whether they are conscious of them or not. Many families grieve because they miss the way the family was before the separation. They don't think about the fact that families are always in a state of change, even without military separations. Natural changes within a family occur so gradually that few members are aware of them.

Because family changes that occur as a result of military separation are often more sudden and unwelcome than life's normal progressive changes, they are harder to accept. Families may feel like separations are interruptions to life rather than changes in life. After the interruption, family life is expected to go back to what it was before. In reality, that seldom, if ever, happens.

A wife may have had to learn to change the oil in the car for the first time when her husband was gone, and after learning how to do that she doesn't know why she was afraid of doing it or uncomfortable doing it before, so she may continue to change the oil in her car after her husband is back home again, not realizing that he is expecting her to want him to do it for her. The wife's growth (in car care and in other areas) could make the husband wonder if he is still needed.

Human sensitivities can make us misinterpret actions of family members and bring us to the wrong conclusions. That's why, especially after a long period of separation, family members need time to adjust to being together again and time to devote attention to understanding each other's feelings. Families should expect a time of adjustment without fearing that it will be traumatic. Don't expect family life to be perfect after a military separation. It wasn't perfect before the separation. Everyone has to adjust his or her thinking and behavior. It may help to talk about the deployment. You may want to reread letters together or talk about specific differences in the way the home operated.

Without realizing it, family members may have put Dad on a pedestal. The tendency to glamorize Dad's military service is natural, because it comes from love for him and missing the good things about him. As the family misses Dad they tend to minimize or forget his weaknesses or bad habits. But when he returns, he will probably still have them and the other family members will have their weaknesses too. At first the family will be so excited to be together that they will be able to ignore each other's irritations and want to party.

Families should celebrate being together again. Party and enjoy each other after the time apart. We have family parties when our family reunites. The rule with our family parties is that we only eat junk food (hot dogs, pizza, snack food, etc.) and each family member gets to choose a game we all play together. It may take an afternoon or evening to play all of the chosen games, and the extended time together adds to the feeling of celebration as well as providing time for us to re-connect. Lots of casual conversation occurs during the games that helps Dad in his re-entry into the family. Without formally talking about it, we end up briefing Dad about how things were done while he was gone, and helping him understand what the boys are interested in now.

In *The Business Traveling Parent,* Dan Verdick suggests ideas for family celebrations. Make your family homecoming celebration fun! After a reasonable time, you will realize that you have celebrated long enough. That length of time depends on the individual family and the length of their separation.

As the transition to a more normal lifestyle occurs, you'll begin to think about what you expect for the family as a whole and for each individual, and examine whether the expectations are realistic. Of course, it's hard to be objective when the family has been separated for a long time, and the excitement of the reunion can cloud the objectivity that is there. There are some expectations that most families will have in common.[1]

What Families Should Expect as They Reunite

To understand the changes that take place while the family is separated, each person in the family may want to answer these questions and share the answers with the rest of the family:

What do I hope has not changed?

What do I know has changed and will be different?

What am I worried about most as we get together again?

What specific problems do I think this separation might have caused in our family?

How do I think our family will respond to being together again?

How will our lives be different because of this deployment?

As you think about those questions and others you may think of that apply to your family, there are some things you can expect as you prepare for your family's reunion:

- Expect the love of your family to be as strong as it was before the separation.
- Expect excitement and celebration, even overwhelming joy, when he arrives.
- Expect married couples to want romantic time alone. Try to take leave time both with the children and just as a couple, if possible.

- Everyone in the family should be free to tell those they've been apart from how much they missed them. People like to hear that someone missed them. Tell them often.
- Expect to see changes in the emotional and physical stamina of each family member.
- Family problems will not disappear during family separations. If children have trouble in school or you are short of money before the deployment, you can expect the problems to still be there.
- Expect some sadness or depression after the initial excitement of the homecoming wears off. If any member of the family individually or the family as a whole has trouble sharing feelings and adjusting to the changes that have taken place, don't be afraid to ask for help. Sometimes a few observations by a competent counselor are all it takes to enable families to work through the adjustment.
- Expect the adjustment to take time. If the separation has been long, the family will need more than a week or two to adjust.
- Expect each family member to need private time and space to think and adjust to the reunion.
- Expect friends and relatives to be anxious to see your husband. If friends and relatives want to visit, make sure you have enough time to reunite as a family *before* you have company. You might need to ask people to wait a few weeks to visit. Family comes first.
- Expect the reunion to be most satisfying if everyone is flexible.
- Expect change and be ready to do things differently rather than resist changes that will occur.
- Your family may not have the same attitude toward your military career as they did before you left. You may want to talk about how they feel about it now.

EXPECTATIONS FOR SPOUSES AT HOME

- Expect to have mixed feelings before your husband gets home. You may be excited about seeing each other but unsure about how it will feel to be together again, and you may wonder what has changed. In the excitement of being together again, you may want to make everything perfect, as if you were going to entertain a celebrity, but maybe your budget won't allow for extra expenses.
- You may wonder whether your husband will look the same and fit into the family in the same way as before the separation. Will he approve of the way the household has been run in his absence?
- Expect your husband to have changed. Realize that you have changed, too. If you know specific ways you have changed, discuss them with your husband.
- If your husband has been far away from home, expect him to have jet lag, and need time to physically adjust to your time zone.
- Your husband may feel emotionally let down or think you don't understand what he's been through.
- Expect your husband to want you to recognize the stress he had while he was gone. Both of you had stress. Don't give in to the temptation to think you had it harder than he did. Support each other. Allow each other to talk. Listening is an act of love.
- Don't schedule too many activities. Expect your family to need time alone to relax. You know what the budget can handle, so don't plan to spend extra money on homecoming celebrations unless you can afford to.
- If your husband has been in a dangerous area, he may be exceptionally quiet or sensitive. Expect that he will need time to open up. Be patient. He may not be ready for a structured routine right away.
- Expect to feel concern about when he may be deployed again.

- It's possible that sexual closeness may be awkward at first. Think of your sexual reunion as a honeymoon, and be sensitive to your husband.
- Expect to want to make up for lost time.
- Reassure your husband of your love; tell him you love him.
- You may wonder whether he was faithful to you while he was gone or whether he missed you. Maintaining good communication throughout the separation can make these concerns avoidable.
- Expect your husband to need to know that your family still needs him. You've managed without him for a long time, and he may wonder whether you can get along as well without him. Make sure he knows that even though you've been able to get through the deployment without him at home, you don't *want* to be separated, and are happy you're together again.
- Expect your husband to wonder how or whether he still fits into the family. Be aware of the fact that your children may come to you for everything and ignore Dad.
- Expect your husband to feel rejected or hurt if children hold back from him. Expect to have to help him understand the best way to approach your young children. There weren't any children deployed with him, and he may not remember everything he knows about relating to children without your gentle reminder.
- Expect that your spouse may want to step right in to handle all of the family's responsibilities again. Talk about how to handle family responsibilities and give it time to develop.
- Expect that it will be hard for you to give up your sole control of the family to share it with your husband.
- Expect your husband not to notice some of the adjustments you need to make because he is home again. He wasn't there, so he doesn't know how things went in his absence.
- You may feel like you no longer have much time for yourself. That's because you've become used to being alone more often during the separation; you need time to adjust to being together and still having some personal time.

- You may get tired of hearing your husband tell people about his deployment experiences. Listen patiently and with interest.

EXPECTATIONS FOR THE DEPLOYED SPOUSE

- Don't develop fantasies or unrealistic expectations about what your homecoming will be like.
- Expect to miss the excitement or glamour of the deployment. Don't expect your family to think of you as a hero because of what you did on the deployment. To them, your absence meant hardship and inconvenience, and although they appreciate your job and are proud of you, they aren't likely to see your deployment as out of the ordinary.
- Expect to feel concern about being deployed again.
- Realize that you may have changed while you were gone. If you know specific ways you have changed, you may want to discuss them with your wife.
- Soon after you get home, go to the commissary, exchange, and gas station to get an idea of what the prices of routine items are. This will help you understand any changes that may have been necessary in the household budget. Expect to have some concerns about the family budget.
- You may feel like no one understands what you've been through.
- You may feel emotional letdown after you get home.
- You may think other peoples' concerns seem petty because of what you've been through.
- Expect to be treated like a guest when you come home. Enjoy your family's attention and celebrate being together.
- Expect that you will need to talk about your experiences.
- Expect your wife to be a little jealous that you have been able to travel places she has never been. Be sensitive about describing where you were.

- It's possible that sexual closeness may be awkward at first. Think of your sexual reunion as a honeymoon, and be sensitive to your wife. Court her.
- Tell your wife you love her often to reaffirm your relationship.
- You may wonder whether your wife was faithful to you while you were gone or whether she missed you. Good communication throughout the separation can make these concerns avoidable.
- Expect your wife to be more independent.
- Your wife may have new friends.
- If your wife was involved in a support group when you were gone, she may ask you to go to meetings with her. Don't hesitate to go.
- Expect your wife to want you to recognize the stress she had while you were gone. Both of you had stress. Don't give in to the temptation to think you had it harder than she did. Support each other and listen to each other.
- Expect to want to make up for lost time. You can't replace the time you were apart, so go slowly and start over instead of trying to make up for your time apart.
- Expect your wife to have new skills or possibly a new job since you left. Find ways to encourage her and let her know you're proud of her. Think about her needs and show her that her activities and interests are important to you.
- You may feel like a stranger in your own home at first, but you will soon fit in again.
- You may not notice that your return is causing adjustment for your family, *but it is*. Try to pay attention to what adjustments are being made.
- Expect changes to occur at home. Your household probably ran differently in your absence, and you may not know how things are done now. Observe for yourself and ask your wife what family routines are like now. Knowing what to expect will help you fit into the routine as everyone adjusts to your homecoming.

- Try not to come home and take control of everything right away. Take time to see how the family managed without you, and ease back into your roles. The family had to do everything while you were away, and probably managed quite well in your absence. If decisions were made that you would have handled differently, remember that those decisions were probably made under stress and your family might not have been used to making decisions, so try to be positive. Show appreciation for their management, and talk about how the roles will change now that you are home again. Be patient.
- Expect to wonder whether you handled everything right from a distance while you were gone, as well as upon your arrival back home. You'll probably wonder when things will return to normal. What was normal before your time away will be different from the normal pattern you will establish after your return.
- Enjoy partying and celebrating. Just don't lose your common sense.
- Expect it to be difficult to know what to say to each family member at first. If you have been gone for a long time, you will probably have to ease back into communicating with the family before you feel as intimate with each member as you did before you left. As you have time, talk to and listen to each child and your wife.
- Expect your children to need your reassurance.
- Expect your children to continue the habits they developed while you were gone. They may not remember to ask you if they want to do something, but go only to your wife. It will take time for them to remember that now they can ask you as well as your wife for permission to do things. If your children come to you first, try to find out how things were done while you were gone before you respond to their requests, so you don't give them different rules than your wife does or contradict her answers.
- Expect to see growth and change in your children. They won't be just like they were when you left. They may have new interests or skills.

- Your friends may seem different than they were before you left.

Coming Home to a Baby

If your wife gave birth to a child while you were gone, your relationship will be very different when you return, especially if the baby is your first child. You may need to talk about how to share the joy of your child and the responsibilities of parenthood. To ease your transition into your new family, you may want to consider the following:

- Ease in slowly. Ask your wife for hints about how to relate to and care for the baby.
- Remember how your wife last described the baby's stage of growth and abilities, so you have an idea of what the baby is like.
- Try to be realistic about what you expect of the baby and your wife. Your wife may be tired and in need of relief. The baby may cry a lot.
- They will be happy to see you, and that may make your reunion seem perfect. Try to be helpful and concentrate on the joy, rather than the extra work or loss of freedom that may result from having a new baby.
- Small babies will need lots of cuddling, skin contact, and time to study your face and eyes.
- If your child is seven months of age or older, he or she may need more time to accept you because you seem like a stranger to him or her.
- Expect that you and your wife will handle and care for the baby differently. As long as you don't handle the baby too roughly, that's OK. The baby will enjoy getting to know you and the way you relate to him or her.
- You may be frustrated about what you've missed in your baby's life while you were gone. If you can be patient and persistent, you will establish your relationship to the child and will feel caught up in time.

CHILDREN'S FEELINGS AND REUNION

Children may not be aware of their emotional needs or understand the changes that take place when Daddy is home again. You may want to read them books that relate family changes and transitions in a manner they can identify with. You may want to consider these ideas:

- Don't expect children to be miniature adults. They may respond to your return in childish ways.
- Babies born during the deployment or less than a year old will probably not know who Daddy is, and may cry when he holds them, or pull away from him. Hug and hold them as much as you can, and become involved in bathing and feeding them.
- Children between 1 and 3 years of age may be unsure about Daddy and avoid him, hide from him, or be slow to approach him. Don't force holding them or showing them affection. If you give them space and time to warm up to you they will. Sit at their level and relate to them in a gentle and fun way.
- Children 3 to 5 years old may be afraid of Daddy or have feelings of guilt about making him go away. They may talk a lot to bring you up to date or misbehave to get your attention. Listen to them and accept their feelings. If you play with them and ask them to show you what new programs they like on TV or what their favorite books are, they will sense your reinforcement of your love for them.
- Children 6 to 12 years old may want a lot of Dad's time and attention. They may dread your return out of fear they will be disciplined. At the same time, they may boast about how proud they are of you. Draw closer to them by looking at their schoolwork with them, looking at family pictures, and praising them whenever you can. Try not to criticize them.
- Teenagers may be excited, moody or act like they don't care about the reunion. They may feel guilty because they're afraid they didn't live up to your expectations while you were gone.

They will wonder how your return will affect their responsibilities and the household rules, and may not want to change anything to accommodate you. Listen to them without judging them. Don't tease them about fashion, style, or music. Respect their privacy. Try to get to know their friends. Share what happened to you while you were gone and ask your teenagers to share what they did while you were gone.

- Children of any age might feel guilty about not living up to Dad's expectations. This can especially be true if they were warned as they were disciplined that there would be consequences when Dad got home.

- Resist the urge to take over disciplining the children right away. They're used to their mother's style of discipline and need time to adjust to your presence before you begin to do a lot of the discipline. Go easy on them for a while.

- Children may feel caught between loyalties for Mom and Dad. Some children may resent Dad because he replaced them in Mom's affections.

- Expect to take time to talk to and listen to children. It will take time to regain their trust and closeness. Do something with each child individually that they will enjoy. Maybe they'd like to repeat the special activity you did with them before you deployed. They may need extra time alone with Mom and with Dad.

- Remember that the children are adapting to the change in routine since Dad got home, and change is stressful for them. You may want to ease up on some of the rules and try not to be too rigid about things that aren't very important.

---

1. The expectations listed include information from the following sources: *Straight Talk: JTF Support Hope Newsletter,* No. 3, 19 August 1994: 2; *Strategies for Healthy Coping with Operational Stress: Humanitarian Operations: Operation Support Hope,* U. S. Army Medical Research Unit-Europe: 6,7; *Relink: Growing Together After Being Apart,* June 1991, USAF Chaplain Service Resource Board: 4; and *Military Chaplains' Review,* Transitions (Winter 1991): 22–28.

· 4 ·
Dissolving Reunion Tension

Thinking about expectations before your husband gets home will help prepare your family for a smoother transition from coping with the separation to living as a complete family again. Often wives whose husbands have been deployed have become more independent and self-confident than they were before the separation. They've had to do many things they weren't used to doing for the family, and feel good about their ability to cope with the added responsibilities.

When their husbands return home, wives may find it hard to give the leadership of the family back to their husbands. Denise McColl says, "It's difficult, but necessary! Children are involved in this entire transition and are observing just how the . . . marriage operates, not to mention the other onlookers who are observing our adjustments (whether we want them to or not). Others will either be encouraged and inspired by us, or discouraged and disillusioned . . ."[1] If you are in a position of leadership and are also experiencing homecoming from a deployment, you may need to help others with their transitions as you try to reunite your own family.

Successfully reuniting families requires sensitivity to each family member's feelings and needs. If religious faith guided the family as they went through the separation, their shared faith may enable them to adjust during the homecoming transition as they look to God for what they need rather than relying on their expectations of what they want each other to do or to be. If you think about how your actions or what you say will sound to your family, you may be more careful about how you act or what you say.

"This is where a sensitive wife must help her husband to understand that being *able* to get along without him is very different from *wanting* to get along without him!"[2] Both spouses have changed over the time of the separation, and the "months of changes may be tough to take all at once. But you can't go back. Accept the new person your spouse is"[3] as you get to know him.

Think back to when you were first married and you wanted to learn as much as you could about each other and make each other happy. See the reunion as a new beginning to your relationship. Think about what made you fall in love with your husband or wife. What attracted you to him or her? You now have the advantage of shared experience, so as you rebuild your relationship you can incorporate good times from your past.

As you discover changes that have taken place in each other and the marriage, decide to find a way to see them as positive improvements rather than disruptions. For example, wives are often much more independent than they were before a military separation. When their husbands return, they feel torn between enjoying their new sense of accomplishment and capability and the need to restore their husbands in their role at home. If both spouses realize that because she had to do everything she gained more of a sense of leadership, neither has to be threatened by it. The deployment has helped the wife develop, and both spouses can appreciate this growth while they sort out how they will share the household responsibilities now that he has returned.

Before my husband deployed, when I needed gas in my car, I'd ask him to fill it up, and he'd do it for me. I learned to do it myself after he left, and I also learned to get the oil changed. Then I wondered why I hadn't been comfortable doing those things earlier. When Ren came home, I was so used to getting gas that I just did it, and I even got the oil changed one day after he returned. He wondered whether I still needed him, and felt left out.

After Dan and I both got used to driving Ren's car, Dan asked me whether he could drive Dad's car to school. I thought that was reasonable, so gave him permission. Ren came home during the school year, in March. The first day after Ren's return, Dan went off to school, like he always did. Ren decided to go somewhere later in the morning, and said, "Where's my car?"

"Dan's got it at school," I replied.

"When did that start?" We thought we'd told Ren everything while he was gone, but apparently we forgot to tell him Dan was driving the car to school. Now that Dad was home, who would drive the car? We had to sort that out.

If you had a family change of command ceremony before Dad left, you may want to have another one now that he's back. This can help sort out the family responsibilities and begin the shift to make Dad part of daily activities again. If you choose to do that, it may be helpful to have a family meeting to draw up lists of responsibilities and distribute them among family members. You can call it your planning meeting for the change of command, held to be sure the ceremony will be a success. Children might enjoy taking part in listing responsibilities, planning the ceremony, and planning a reception for after the family ceremony. Make it a fun event.

1. McColl, *Footsteps,* 137.
2. Moritz, Beverly. *Service Separations: A Wife's Perspective.*: (Englewood, CO: Officer's Christian Fellowship), 14.
3. Hicks, Robert M. *Returning Home.* (Tarrytown, NY: Fleming H. Revell Company, 1991), 109.

· 5 ·

WELCOMING SINGLE SERVICE MEMBERS HOME

Military members who are married are usually welcomed home by their families, but who welcomes single service members when they come back from deployment? Many single members have friends that welcome them, but they may miss their families as they see family members embracing their married friends to welcome them home. If you have a single friend who is returning after a deployment, you may want to think of ways to make her or him feel the warmth of a family greeting. Here are a few ideas you may want to consider:

- Make a sign or banner to welcome your friend home.
- Decorate your friend's room, car, apartment or house with balloons, ribbons, or flowers.
- Surprise your friend with his or her favorite snacks.
- One unit in Schweinfurt, Germany, went to the single soldiers' rooms and made their beds, turned down the sheets, and left mints on their pillows. They also put bags of cookies, gum, candy, instant soups, and food at the foot of each bed.[1]
- Throw a "Welcome Home" party.
- Ask your friend to tell you about the experiences of the deployment.

- Tell your friend you missed him or her and are happy he or she is back.

1. Barham, J. P. "Helicopter scouts, engineers return to Germany," *Stars and Stripes*. 23 November 1996; 4.

· 6 ·
Reunion Resources

Resources for Families

- **The Business Traveling Parent**
  How to Stay Close to Your Kids When You're Far Away
  by Dan Verdick
  Mr. Verdick includes activities to do with your children before you leave, while you're gone, and when you get back home. He also gives resources to expand on some of his ideas.
  Published by Robins Lane Press, Beltsville, MD. www.robinslane.com
  Available at bookstores. If the bookstore near you does not have it, ask them to order it.

- **Today's Military Wife: Meeting the Challenges of Service Life**
  by Lydia Sloan Cline
  Available at bookstores; published by Stackpole Books.

- **Heroes at Home: Help & Hope for America's Military Families**
  by Ellie Kay

- **Published by The Bureau For At-Risk Youth:**
  Titles in the Family Forum Library—Military Edition:
  Deployment and Reunion: Challenges and Opportunities
  Stress and the Military Family
  Loss and Change in the Military Family
  Communication Skills for the Military Family
  Coloring Book:
  Welcome Home!
  Available from your Family Support Center, your chaplain, or
  the publisher:
  The Bureau For At-Risk Youth
  135 Dupont Street
  P.O. Box 760
  Plainview, NY 11803-0760
  (800) 99-YOUTH
  e-mail: info@at-risk.com
  www.at-risk.com

- **Published by Channing L. Bete Co.:**
  Let's Talk About Reunion; an information and activities book
  Your Parent is Coming Home; a coloring and activities book
  Stress Management
  Parents and Stress
  What You Should Know About Stress and Your Child
  About Reunion
  MISSION: READINESS: A Personal and Family Guide
  Available from your Family Support Center, your chaplain or
  the publisher:
  Scriptographic Booklets
  Channing L. Bete Co. Inc.
  200 State Road
  South Deerfield, MA 01373-0200
  (800) 477-4776
  e-mail: custsvcs@channing-bete.com
  www.channing-bete.com

Army Resources

*   *Family Redeployment Reunion Home Study Guide*
    Personal Redeployment Readiness Guide
    Part of the USAREUR and Seventh Army Personal Redeployment Readiness Plan.

Navy Workshops and Programs

*   **Return and Reunion**
    Return and Reunion includes workshop and support group meetings for families of deployed personnel. Some of the meetings target children. Families learn to understand expectations each family member has for reuniting the family. Counseling and Ombudsman support is also available. A parallel program is conducted aboard returning ships to discuss topics that include reestablishing family intimacy, financial planning, and setting goals.

*   **Shipboard Return and Reunion**
    A team from the Navy Family Support Center comes aboard the ship during the transit home from an extended deployment to present a workshop on family, children, and financial issues. The emphasis is placed on making a good thing better as the family is reunited. The workshop is presented during the last month at sea.

*   **Homecoming Program**
    In a discussion format, preparations for reunion are presented by addressing emotional aspects of reunion and changes that may occur upon return. In some areas a play, *Coming Home Again* is featured as part of the program, which is presented just before the return date.

RESOURCES FOR PEOPLE IN SUPPORT OF MILITARY FAMILIES

- *Reunion! Training Resources for the Unit Ministry Team*
  Department of the Army, Office of the Chief of Chaplains

- *Rebonding and Rebuilding*
  A reunion seminar
  USAREUR and 7th Army
  Part of the USAREUR and Seventh Army Personal Redeployment Readiness Plan

- *Caring for Military Families*
  by David A. Paap
  Order from: Stephen Ministries
                  2045 Innerbelt Business Center Dr.
                  St. Louis, MO 63114-5765
                  (314) 428-2600
                  www.stephenministries.com

IV

SOME DON'T RETURN

· 1 ·

WE REGRET TO
INFORM YOU . . .

Some families who send loved ones off on deployments don't have the happiness of reunion at the completion of the duty. According to DOD statistics, an average of two thousand service members have died each year for the last fifteen years. That means about five military deaths occur every day.[1] Deployed servicemen and women face the possibility that they may not return, and so must their families.

One wife said, "God forbid, if anything should happen to where he will not be returning, my comment will be that Daddy died doing what is right and protecting his family . . . make the best out of every day that God gives us."[2] She faced the possibility of death with a good attitude. Not all military families have her perspective. Many military members and their families live in denial that anything could ever happen to them. If they don't admit they could die, they don't have to think about it.

Some may think it's a sign of weakness to admit their own mortality. But the fact remains that some military members die while on duty, in accidents, or by hostile action. Some are taken prisoner or are otherwise unaccounted for. ". . . I'd known four pilots lost to bad luck or bad weather or some malfunction that defied the best maintenance in the world. None of them died in combat; it didn't take a war to make our business risky. But until you faced it foursquare, death remained a tragedy that happened to someone else."[3]

Don't let the denial that anything could happen to you prevent your family from talking about and preparing for the possibility that you may not return from duty. If you are taken prisoner or listed as missing, your family may not know where you are or whether you're healthy. The uncertainty can continue for months or years. How do you prepare for that possibility?

Among military couples, those that discuss the possibilities that military members could be killed, taken prisoner, or declared missing in action, ". . . the possibility of something happening, which would prevent the return of the military man, those wives were better able to handle the ambiguous separation. . . . There were predictably fewer problems in coping with the separation."[4] Wives who learn to discount and ignore rumors also have fewer problems. Know who to ask for the truth, and ignore other sources of information as much as possible.

1.   Carroll, Bonnie, Lisa Hudson and Diane Ruby. "Complicated Grief in the Military," in *Living With Grief After Sudden Loss*, ed. Kenneth J. Doka, PH.D.: (Bristol, PA: Taylor & Francis, 1996), 73.
2.   Lauren, Internet chat room at www.parentcenter.com; 9 October 2001.
3.   O'Grady, Captain Scott. *Return With Honor.*: (New York, NY: Doubleday, 1995), 90.
4.   Hunter, Edna J. *Families Under the Flag.*: (New York, NY: Praeger Scientific CBS Educational and Professional Publishing, 1982), 24.

· 2 ·
POW / MIA

To prepare for the possibility of your husband being taken prisoner or listed as missing, you may need to think about many of the same issues you would have to address if he were to die. To help understand them, think a moment about past experiences of military spouses. After the Vietnam conflict, some spouses felt like their husbands had even vanished from the military. Those feelings, combined with the order not to talk about their situations publicly, led some of the wives of Vietnam-era POW and MIA service members to form two organizations to bring their concerns to public attention.

The National League of Families of American Prisoners and Missing in Southeast Asia began in the late 1960s when the wife of a prisoner thought the government was wrong to tell the families not to tell their stories publicly. The first POW/MIA story was published in 1968. That publication resulted in wives networking and forming a group that led to the National League of Families. The League is still active today.

The National Military Family Association (NMFA) began in 1969. Military wives and widows lobbied for financial security and benefits for survivors of service members. The NMFA is now a strong voice for military families in Washington. Its work has resulted in government policies that affect Active Duty families as well as surviving families and retirees.

Today it may not seem likely that service members will be taken POW or listed as MIA. However, the peacekeeping missions in various parts of the world, regional conflicts we become engaged in, and the threat of terrorism make both the POW and the MIA status for servicemen and women possible. Today's military family should discuss those possibilities as well as the possibility of death. Preparing your family for the possibility of your death will also equip them for the possibility that you could be missing in action or taken prisoner.

It's hard for a wife to prepare for how she will go on if she doesn't know when or if her husband will return. "From personal experience, I will go on record as saying that the thing that kept me going when he was a POW . . . was **FAITH.** Faith in him, faith in myself, and, above all, faith in a higher being."[1] The uncertainty of the husband's welfare can also make it more difficult to help children understand what is happening to Daddy. But uncertainty also gives the family room to hope that Daddy will return.

Barbara Eberly, whose husband was a prisoner of war in 1991, encourages wives in that situation to "keep their faith in our system, our government, their husbands, and themselves."[2] Colonel (Ret.) David Eberly adds that he would tell captives to concentrate on resisting, staying alive, and not to worry about their families.[3] The Eberly's religious faith, support at their base, and hope to see the family reunited brought them through their experience. Each family facing POW/MIA status has to make a conscious decision not to give up hope that the family will be reunited.

Yet, how long can a family hold out hope when there appears to be no end to the uncertainty of the husband's status or return? Holding out hope is different than going on with life. Some wives whose husbands were taken prisoner or declared missing during the Vietnam War have still not received information about their husbands. Some of them may still hope to see their husbands return.

They have all found ways to go on with their lives during the uncertainty though. Edna Hunter says that, "wives who had closed out the husband's role (that is, made decisions and took actions as if the husband were no longer in the family) actually coped better than those who did not . . ."[4] They found the strength to make decisions they had to make as they hoped for their husband's return. You will also be able to find that strength if it's necessary.

The strength to hope for his return may come in unexpected ways. If your husband is held prisoner, he may not be able to correspond with you, but it's possible to get a message through.

> One captured pilot . . . followed the Iraqi script and unemotionally mumbled a few words of propaganda into the television camera. But then, he seized the chance to add those otherwise mundane words: "Honey, I love you. Tell the kids to study hard." In four short words a husband assured a waiting wife that no matter how many miles separated them, and no matter what danger threatened him, his love for her was the first priority in his mind. In six more words, the children were reminded that they still had a dad, that he wanted them to work hard, to achieve the most they could.[5]

Essentially, he asked his family to remember him while they carried on their daily lives. If you should face those circumstances, it will be best if you maintain your daily routines, too. You may not want to plan for more than a few days, weeks, or months at a time, but you'll have to go on with life while you wait for news about your husband.

Your relatives will also be waiting for word about him, so you'll probably want to stay in close communication with them. They may encourage you. Whether you find support from them or elsewhere, you'll need someone to talk to who will understand how you feel. You may find that understanding in a relative, friend, your husband's unit, the chapel or church you attend, or a service organization. Think about where you receive encouragement and support.

When many people are in stressful situations, they are helped most by others who have experienced the same thing they're going through. You may want to contact the National League of Families of American Prisoners and Missing in Southeast Asia for advice and support (see the Support Group Information section of the resources that follow this section for information about how to contact them).

Studies of families separated in uncertain circumstances during the Vietnam War gave researchers the information they needed to give suggestions to help families who would face the same uncertainty in the future. They emphasize the importance of an "outreach program from the very beginning because that is when the need for support from others is the greatest."[6] The stress wives face can be eased a lot if they meet other women in the same situation as they are in. They also need a place where they can talk about their frustrations. There they can benefit from the advice and experiences of women who have been in the same situation before, or for a longer time.

Research confirms the idea that the military should not lose contact with families, but continue to support them and give them information until the status of their husbands has been resolved or they have returned.[7] If your husband is a POW or MIA and you want to talk with someone who has been a POW, or the spouse of a former POW, contact your Casualty Assistance Office or the National League of Families.

If your husband is listed POW or MIA, you'll receive an official message from the Casualty Assistance Officer. They, or your installation Public Affairs Office, will give you advice about how to respond to media inquiries and tell you what information you are free to share with the public. You should call relatives who may be contacted by media to let them know what should or should not be said. What families say *can* have a direct affect on how a POW is treated. Keep the Public Affairs Office or Casualty Assistance Office informed about any contact you have with the media.

Some specific things to remember if your loved one is POW or MIA are the following:

- You may feel upset, tired, lose your appetite, have trouble sleeping, or be preoccupied. These are normal responses to your situation. It's OK to be sad.
- Expect to wonder whether you should have said or done something more for and with your husband before he left.
- Expect to experience different stages of grief after learning of his status.
- Expect news of his welfare to be irregular and non-specific for an indefinite period of time.
- If pictures of your husband are shown on TV by his captors, try to take comfort in knowing he is alive and knows you will likely be seeing the broadcast, even though he may not be allowed to speak. See any communication as a connection that draws you together and points to your reunion.
- Determine to be a survivor, as well as expect that he will survive. When her husband was MIA in Vietnam, and a year later when she knew he was POW, Myrna Borling said that it helped her to think about their past together, and the future together, even though she couldn't think about the present. As her daughter grew from the baby her husband left into the seven-year-old she was when he returned, Myrna talked about Daddy to keep him in the family and be sure the girl knew who her father was.[8] You, like Myrna, can get through, one day at a time if necessary.
- Try to keep up your normal routine as much as you can.
- Eat balanced meals.
- Don't turn to alcohol or drugs.
- Get enough sleep. Exercise regularly.
- It may help you to talk to other people who have been in your situation.
- Continue with family vacations and activities you would normally be involved in.
- You may gain strength through your religious faith and church group. Allow them to support you.
- Don't wait next to the phone for news every day. If there is new information, you will know it as soon as it is available.

- You may want to keep a journal during this time.

Children of POW/MIA

If your husband is a captive or missing your children may worry about him and may be confused or afraid. They will hear parts of conversations, and may jump to wrong conclusions. To help them, you may want to consider the following:[9]

- Small children may not understand what happened apart from the fact that Daddy is gone and they miss him. They will sense the emotional strain around them, especially in Mommy.
- Children may think Daddy left home because they were naughty, and now they are being punished. They may feel guilty and responsible. You may want to talk to them and tell them that sometimes children feel like it's their fault, but that is not true. Then tell them what happened in terms they can understand.
- Explain to your children what it means to be a prisoner of war or missing in action. They need to understand that Dad didn't do anything wrong and is not like a criminal in jail.
- Be prepared to talk about rumors your children may hear from their friends.
- If watching news on TV bothers your children, limit their exposure to it.
- Children may fear that since Dad is already missing something bad will also happen to Mom.
- Children may over-identify with Dad, pretending to be him in the kind of captivity they imagine he is in.
- Children may react with anger, fear, resentment, guilt, or anxiety. They need to know that those are normal ways to respond under the circumstances.
- Children will feel more secure and stable if you maintain their regular routines.
- Children may cry a lot, have nightmares, rebel, become shy, bite their nails, or become afraid of the dark. They may lose

interest in schoolwork or misbehave in school. All of these behaviors can be reactions to Dad's status. Don't neglect necessary discipline, but try to show them that you love them more often, be more understanding, and give them the attention they need.

- Don't give the oldest child responsibility that he or she is not ready for. He or she should not be asked to fill the role of man or lady of the house.
- Children look to you for guidance. They watch how you react and imitate your behavior in their own ways.
- Don't make promises you can't keep. You shouldn't tell them you are sure Dad will come home.
- Children need someone to talk to and a safe place to vent frustrations. Be open and honest with them, and communicate freely within your family.
- Don't hide your feelings or tears from your children. Teach them by example that strong people talk to their families about what's bothering them so they don't feel alone. When we all know how the others feel we can help each other through the hard times.
- If you need help supporting your children, ask your Family Support Center, your chaplain, or your church. They will be happy to help you or refer you to the help you need.

1. Moore, Eva J. Letter to author, 8 November 1996.
2. Glenn, Mike. "Former prisoner advises POWs to concentrate on staying alive," *Air Force Times*, 19 April 1999; 24.
3. Ibid.
4. Hunter, Edna, 66.
5. Bauer, Gary L. "Let's Go Home Again," *Focus on the Family*. October 1992; 2.
6. Hunter, Edna, 69.
7. Ibid., 71.
8. Interview with author, 16 September, 1999.
9. Some ideas are taken from "Surviving the Tough Times: A Guide For Families of POWs/MIAs," Army Community and Family Support, Department of the Army; 5–6.

· 3 ·

WHAT IF YOUR SPOUSE COMES BACK, BUT A FRIEND DOESN'T?

Your spouse may come back safely but one of your military friends may not return. If a friend dies, you may experience grief as intense as if you've lost a relative. The death of a friend can be a sudden reminder that you could have been the one to die or lose your spouse.

If a friend dies you will probably want to show your care and sympathy to his widow and family. You may wonder what you can say to convey your feelings. You may not know how to help them. The best thing you can do is to continue to be a friend. If you don't know what to say, it's OK to tell them that, hug them, and just be there without talking. They will probably be in a state of shock and may not know what they want or need, but your presence will be a comfort to them.

People react to death in a variety of ways. Some become angry, and don't know how to express their feelings. Others become moody, talkative, or lash out at those who are trying to support them. Love and stand with your friend regardless of how he or she reacts to the trauma of death. Immediately after a person has been notified of the death of their spouse they need the freedom to react in whatever way is natural for them, and to know that their friends are there and accept their response to the death without judgment.

You may be able to reassure her by reminding her that mixed-up emotions and difficulty trying to focus her attention are normal responses to death. As the grieving spouse faces the reality of the death, she may be able to tell you how you can help her. Before she is able to express specific requests for help, you can still help her if you are sensitive to her needs and willing to offer assistance.

Helping a Friend During Grief

When you hear that a friend has died, be sure the information you have is correct before you tell anyone. You may want to call the surviving spouse to ask her if what you heard is true, and to offer your help. Your friend will appreciate specific offers of help; she is probably not able to think about details since her mind is numb with grief. If you want to help a grieving friend, you may want to consider the following ideas:[1]

- Offer to make phone calls for her, and if she accepts your offer ask her what she wants you to say. When you make the calls, don't use too much detail, but calmly tell them what they need to know. Allow them time to absorb the news and ask them if they know others who should be notified. Keep the calls focused and short.
- Offer to clean house for her, or just pitch in and clean if she is close enough to you that she would be comfortable with it.
- Answer the phone for her. Be sure to note who called, their phone number, date, and message.
- Keep a list of food people may bring over and list what dishes have to be returned to which individuals.
- Baby-sit the children, take them to the park, feed them, or put them to bed.
- Pick up dry cleaning, groceries, mail, etc.
- Pick up people from the airport and find them a place to stay.
- Help select clothes for the funeral and do shopping that may be necessary.

- Help make travel arrangements for relatives, or for your friend if the funeral will be held in another area.
- Offer to go along to the funeral home to make the arrangements.
- Offer to call the chaplain or minister.
- Ask if there will be a reception at the church or their home after the funeral. Offer to help organize and plan it.
- Make yourself available to talk.
- Ask questions that require more than a yes or no answer. Avoid doing a lot of talking or telling your friend what to do.
- Be a good listener. Let your friend talk about her husband if she wants to.
- Don't try to reassure your friend by saying things like "you're still young, and I'm sure you'll find another husband." She wants her husband, not a replacement. Understand and respect her feelings.
- Share your memories of the deceased with your friend.
- Let your friend cry and grieve. Don't be afraid to cry with your friend or let your friend see your emotions.
- Encourage your friend to rest.
- Don't keep your friend so busy that she avoids her grief. She needs comfort and time to absorb and work through her loss, not extra activity.
- Don't make decisions for your friend.
- Don't encourage your friend to become too dependent on you.
- Don't dominate your friend's time.
- Patiently repeat information that may not sink in the first time your friend hears it.
- Help your friend to pace herself.
- Visit her regularly after the funeral when the activity is slowing down.
- Ask your friend if she wants you to help her write thank you notes or address envelopes for them.
- Suggest that your friend become involved in a support group. Tell her if you hear of seminars or workshops that may help or interest her.

1. Many of the ideas listed come from *The Mourning Handbook*, by Helen Fitzgerald, pages 270–280.

· 4 ·

DEATH NOTIFICATION

The way you hear about the death of your spouse will be an important part of your response to the news. With today's on-location television coverage of events, you could be informed of your spouse's death by a news report before the military has a chance to notify you. That kind of notification is obviously traumatic. If your spouse dies in an event that is reported on the news, you may be besieged by reporters who want to interview the family and your privacy may be compromised.

Notoriety makes grief more difficult for the family because their personal grief processes are complicated by and interrupted by the attention focused on them. They may be confused emotionally, waiting for official confirmation or notification of the death, and holding out some hope that their loved one is still alive. "Once the deceased becomes a public persona entering the public domain, families have lost yet another part of that person during a time that they have not learned how to cope with their initial loss. Since the nature of news is what is 'new,' the pace in which the press intrudes in the victims' families is uncaring and often quite relentless."[1] It's better for families to have time to absorb the shock of the death before they're faced with public attention.

If your spouse dies while on Active Duty, you can expect to be notified in the following manner:

- The duty officer receives news of the death and assembles a Casualty Notification Team (CNT) made up of the Casualty Assistance Officer (CAO) or Casualty Assistance Calls Officer (CACO), a chaplain, and a medical representative.
- The CNT comes to your home and the CAO introduces himself and the other members of the team.
- The CAO tells you what happened and gives you the official Notification Letter.
- The CNT answers any questions you have and helps you as you react to the news.
- The CAO tells you to expect to be contacted by a military Casualty Assistance Representative (if you are eligible to receive this service), who will visit you within twenty-four hours.
- When the Casualty Assistance Representative meets with you, he or she will explain what benefits are available to you and tell you how to use them.

Some of the military benefits you may be eligible for if your spouse dies are a monthly amount of pay, a lump sum death benefit, ninety days to stay in government housing, an advisor to help you with arrangements and benefits, cremation or embalming, a casket or urn, transportation of remains to final resting place, an American Flag, military honors, burial in a national cemetery, provision of burial arrangements, and a grave headstone or marker.

The notification process is much the same for Active Duty members and Reserve or Guard members who are on Active Duty or deployed. Benefits will vary according to the sponsor's duty status and rank.

1. Cummock, Victoria. "Journey of a Young Widow: The Bombing of Pan Am 103," in *Living With Grief After Sudden Loss*, ed. Kenneth J. Doka, Ph.D.: (Bristol, PA: Taylor & Francis, 1996), 6.

· 5 ·

THE FUNERAL OR
MEMORIAL SERVICE

Many people wonder why it's important to have a funeral or memorial service. The service helps survivors through their grief. The service gives comfort to the grieving, helps them face the reality of the death, and gives a sense of closure to the shock of the death. This enables mourners to say goodbye to the deceased and begin to move on with life again.

Funerals are services at which the remains of the deceased are present. After the service, those who attend may join the procession to the cemetery and the gravesite where the interment will take place. Memorial services are much the same as funeral services, but the body is not present. Usually a picture of the deceased is displayed at a memorial service.

To make a funeral or memorial service most meaningful to those who will grieve your death, you may want to plan for it now. Planning eases the burden for your family if you die suddenly, because they will have fewer decisions to make during the first days the death. You may want to consider the following items as you plan for your funeral or memorial service:

• Is it important that you are buried close to your hometown or relatives?

- Decide what city and cemetery you want to be buried in, and buy a plot.
- Make tentative arrangements if you want to be buried in a National Cemetery. Where is the National Cemetery that is closest to your hometown?
- Can you pick out and pay for a burial marker now? Are you eligible to have a marker placed at your grave at government expense?
- To which funeral home will your remains be sent?
- What kind of casket do you want?
- What kind of service do you want at the funeral home or church?
- Do you want military honors?
- What customs do you or your family or church observe?
- Are there specific songs you would like sung at the service?
- Does your spouse or family want pictures or videos taken of the casket, service, or cemetery?
- Do you want to be cremated? If so, do you want the bone fragments pulverized? What do you want done with your ashes? They can be interred at a cemetery in a columbarium (a wall with recesses for ashes and a place for a plaque marker), taken home in an urn, or scattered in a special place. If you choose to have your ashes scattered or keep them in an urn, will your family want a cenotaph (a monument to honor a dead person whose remains are not available for burial?) Where?[1]
- If your remains were not found and not available for burial, would you like the family to have a memorial service? Where would you want a cenotaph placed?

1. Fitzgerald, Helen. *The Mourning Handbook.*: (New York, NY: Simon and Schuster, 1994), 68–69.

· 6 ·

IF YOUR SPOUSE DIES

If your spouse dies suddenly, you won't be able to prepare for death or say goodbye, as you would if there were a prolonged illness. The shock of an unexpected death makes it even more difficult to accept. When you receive the news you may be numb, cry, or begin thinking of what will happen next. The initial reaction is not necessarily an indication of how you will go through the grieving process.

The amount of support you have will impact how you grieve. It will probably be good for you to talk about your feelings with someone who will listen without trying to influence how you feel. Having people around you that you feel close to will help you remember that you have meaningful relationships that continue, even though you've lost the person you're closest to on earth.

When you're told about the death, ask for the details about how it happened. Those details can help you accept the reality that the death happened. View your spouse's body if it's possible. Facing the reality of the death and the body helps people accept the changes that will occur in their lives. Your spouse's death will result in a lot of changes in your life. You will suddenly be responsible for the provision and nurture of the family. While you assume that new role, you'll still be grieving.

You may wonder how long the grieving process will take. Since everyone handles grief in his or her own unique way and on his or her own timetable, there is no predictable amount of time it should take. One thing everyone has in common is the need to bring closure to a tragic death and to feel like they've said goodbye to the deceased. For some, that closure may come when they see the body. Others may feel closure after the funeral or burial.

You can't prepare yourself to know when closure will occur for you, but you can prepare yourself for the possibility of losing your spouse. Military families may be more prepared for the possibility of losing a spouse than they realize they are. ". . . one woman told me that her husband, a military man, would often be gone for six months at a time. She said she hated those long absences, but found that they helped her to deal with her husband's death."[1] She had learned to make decisions on her own.

You'll have a lot of decisions to make quickly if your husband dies. If you can put any of them off until later, do so. If you live in military housing or overseas when he dies, you can't delay some decisions, like where you'll live. You'll have a limited amount of time to move out of government housing or move back to the States. Try to avoid rushing into decisions about moving too quickly, and avoid moving to escape memories.

PREPARATION FOR A SPOUSE'S DEATH

Some of the things to think about as you prepare yourself for the possibility of your spouse's death are the following:

- Where would you want to live if your spouse died? Would you want to buy a house? How will you make that decision?
- Expect grief to take time.
- Expect it to be difficult to realize that you are a widow or widower.
- Expect to wonder whether life will ever be normal again.

- Expect to have trouble concentrating and remembering things. You may be less organized than you'd normally be. Allow yourself a slower pace for a while.
- Expect to be preoccupied with what faces you and with the shock of your loss.
- Expect to have to remind yourself to get enough rest, eat right, and get some exercise.
- Expect that life will be different and won't return to the way it was before.
- If you have children, you'll have to help them grieve while you are working through your own grief. It's difficult to help someone when you're in need yourself. Planning in advance how to help your children if their other parent dies will equip you to go through the difficult process if it should become necessary. Ideas about helping children follow this discussion.

WHEN DEATH OCCURS

As a military wife, you may not have the established support systems around you that your civilian counterparts have, such as extended family, a church you've belonged to most of your life, long-term friendships, or long-term relationships at work. Military people do support one another, but depending on the length of your assignments, you may not have the depth in your military relationships that you need when your spouse dies. In addition to the uncertain availability of support, a military wife is dependent on the military for information about the death. Sometimes official reports about military deaths are classified and families don't have access to the information.

After the Casualty Assistance has been provided, you may be on your own, seemingly abandoned by the military. "The military widow is coping not only with grief, but with her 'new' life outside the confines and security of the military safety net, which once provided structure and emotional safety to her world. The civilian world, along with grief, is foreign. These are factors documented to predispose the survivor to a more complicated grief."[2] Women who had experienced these things came to realize that military widows often need more support than the military system offers. In response, they formed TAPS (Tragedy Assistance Program for Survivors, Inc.). TAPS is a group of survivors committed to reaching out to help others heal. If your husband dies, you may want to contact TAPS (for information, refer to Support Group Information in the resources that follow this section of the book).

Even if you've done all you can to prepare for the possibility of your spouse's death, it will be a shock if it occurs. No amount of planning can take away the emotional impact of such a tragic loss. You will probably have a flood of emotions as well as things to do and, as a result, you may have trouble trying to accomplish anything. In addition to the preceding preparation, you may want to remember the following concerns as you face the death of your spouse:

- You'll have to decide whether you want to be a survivor or a victim. Choosing to survive will enable you to face what lies ahead.
- Expect your feelings to fluctuate. Grief is not a predictable or orderly process. Expect to use a lot of your energy as you grieve, and do not put your own needs aside.
- Expect to feel overwhelmed with wonder about how you can go on without your husband. Instead of thinking about the long-term, it may help to concentrate on getting through hours, days, and weeks at first.
- Don't try to hide your grief from your children. Try to express it to them in words that show that you love them, and although you are sad that Dad died, you'll feel better soon.
- Get help with running the household while you're adjusting to the death if you need it. Maybe you need to take relatives and friends up on their offers to babysit, cook, clean the house, do the laundry, go to the grocery store, or run errands for you. Don't wait for people to offer to help you; ask for help. Your friends and relatives may be hesitant to volunteer because they don't want to intrude, but they may be ready to help.

- Expect to spend some time reflecting on your marriage and lives together.
- You may feel like all the security in life is gone or that nothing is safe. Don't demand too much of yourself while you're feeling like that. For example, if you aren't comfortable driving, ask someone to help until you feel ready to drive again.
- Shield your children from feelings of despair or wondering how you'll cope with the loss. They need to feel secure in your care. If you need to talk about those feelings, talk to an adult out of the child's earshot. You may want to talk to a counselor or chaplain.
- Don't be in too much of a hurry to dispose of your spouse's clothes and personal belongings. Everything does not have to be done at once.
- Go through your spouse's personal things yourself rather than allowing someone else to dispose of them for you. You may find yourself remembering special moments that you'll cherish as you decide what to do with his things.
- Expect your mind to wander easily, so be careful driving.
- You may not remember all of the details of the funeral and burial afterward.
- Try to develop a new routine or schedule for yourself.
- Set reachable goals.
- Don't turn to drugs or alcohol for comfort.
- Expect holidays and special anniversaries to be filled with memories and emotion. The anticipation could be worse than the pain you think you'll feel though, so don't completely avoid celebrations. You may want to celebrate in a different way than you did in the past. Don't force yourself to keep old traditions alive if you don't want to.
- Expect to need some time to know who you are apart from your spouse.
- You'll have to decide whether you want to wear your wedding ring. Maybe you'll be comfortable replacing it with another ring. Do what is best for you.
- Although it may seem distant, you'll come to a point of release from the emotion of grieving, a little at a time.

- Find a support group (such as TAPS) to participate in, where you'll be with others who have shared your experience.
- How often will you want to visit the grave? You'll probably be shocked when you see the grave marker for the first time with your spouse's name engraved on it. Visiting the grave may help you work through your grief.

1. Fitzgerald, 148.
2. Carroll, Hudson, and Ruby, 76.

· 7 ·

CHILDREN AND DEATH

It's natural to want to shelter children from pain and to try to minimize the effect of death in their lives. Although the intention is understandable, you won't be able to shield them. When you're notified that your husband died, you must decide whether you'll tell the children yourself, have someone else do it, or a combination of both. Your explanation to your children will depend on their ages and levels of understanding. When you tell them, be honest and straightforward, using simple language they will have no trouble understanding.

Children respond to the news of death in a wide variety of ways, just like adults do. However, they may not fully understand what is happening, so their reactions may reveal that confusion. They may imitate the response of the adults around them, become withdrawn, exhibit attention-getting behavior, become angry, deny death's reality, refuse to talk about it, or even want to die to join Daddy. They'll probably be affected most by watching their mother's response to get an idea of how they should act. They probably have no experience with the death of someone they know, and don't know what to expect. Adults can help them by remembering that they need to be told what is happening.

Children sense the emotional pain around them and recognize that something bad happened. They need to know why everyone feels so sad. Rather than let them rely on information they overhear, tell them what's causing the emotion they sense. Someone special is dead. Give them direct answers to their questions. In their book *How Do We Tell the Children?* Dan Schaefer and Christine Lyons list questions that children often ask, giving appropriate answers. They explain that dead means that a person's body won't work or do what it used to do any more.[1] Their answers to questions children often ask may be a great help to a parent or friend who has trouble knowing how to say things in ways children can relate to. Schaefer and Lyons also provide excellent explanations of events connected with death and funerals for children.

Children need to grieve just like adults do. Seeing the body will help them accept the reality of the death, but they should be told first what they'll see. If they don't know what really happened, they will imagine what they think happened, and a child's imagination is usually worse than anything that could have happened. If childhood misunderstandings aren't corrected, they can be carried into adulthood.

A child should be allowed to go to the visitation at the funeral home, the wake, the funeral, and the cemetery if he wants to, but should not be required to go. He should know that people there will be crying and what will happen. He will also be helped by a description of the room and flowers in the funeral home, the casket, the clothes that Daddy is wearing if the body is available for viewing, who will be there, and the service.

Knowing exactly what to expect may help a child decide whether he really wants to go along to the funeral home, wake, or funeral service. Attending the funeral and seeing how adults express their grief will help children learn how to express their own emotion and learn that grieving is a part of life. The funeral also gives children the opportunity to say goodbye to Daddy. They can't go to the funeral later if they change their minds, so it is important to be sure they have the opportunity to attend.

You may want to tell children how different people in the family will act at the funeral. If your children know that Aunt Jane will cry and Uncle Jim will say that real men don't cry, it will help them when they observe those behaviors. Then you will also have a chance to tell them that many adults do not know how to express grief very well, so they say things that aren't exactly true to help themselves feel better, like Uncle Jim will probably do. Tell them that other adults may tell them things to make them feel better. They should remember that what Mom tells them is true, even if some of the adults make it sound mixed-up. Children don't understand everything you do, and they may need more explanations than you think they do.

In addition to their lack of understanding, the whole world of military children is shaken up when their sponsoring parent dies, because they have to leave the military community and lifestyle that they identify with. As a result, they lose the security of a parent and the predictability of their lifestyle at the same time. However, the military lifestyle does help children learn flexibility, which helps them deal with the changes they must face.

HELPING CHILDREN THROUGH GRIEF

It's difficult to prepare children for news as tragic as the death of a parent. It may be more realistic to think about how to help children if death occurs, so that the surviving adults in the children's lives will be prepared to care for children in crisis. If you have the occasion to help your children or the children of a friend when a parent dies, you may want to consider the following:

- Don't assume that children know Daddy will be lying down in the casket.
- It's good for children to see Daddy in the casket, but whatever age your children are, never leave them standing alone at the casket. They need the warmth and support of your presence as they view their dead father.

- Always refer to the deceased by name; don't refer to him as "the body."
- The children need reassurance that they won't be abandoned.
- Children may not understand what is happening, and that may upset them. Try to help them understand.
- Be consistent about keeping your promises to the child. For example, be sure to get home at the time you tell them you'll be back, not later.
- Expect children to ask questions over and over again as the death sinks in. Patiently give them direct answers each time. If it becomes emotionally difficult to answer at the time they ask you a question, ask them if it is OK if you talk about it later, and then don't forget to follow through.
- Try to avoid situations in which the child will feel uncertain. Explain what will happen so they know what to expect if they will be exposed to new experiences.
- If you are the surviving parent, never leave the child without telling him or her. If you'll be getting a sitter, tell the child when you'll be leaving and when you'll return, even if the child will be in bed sleeping at the time.
- Be sure children know who would take care of them or who to call if something happened to you.
- Children may wake up during the night and come to sleep in the parent's bed. Allow the child to feel the comfort of falling asleep next to you, but bring the child back to his or her own bed after he or she is asleep, so he or she will wake up in their own bed. This will help them maintain normal life without showing any rejection.
- Be available when the children need your attention or want to talk, even if you have to drop something to give them your full attention. Let them know they're important to you. Listen to what they say and be sensitive to their feelings.
- If you think the child needs professional help, get it. You can ask your pediatrician, chaplain, or Family Services (or Support) Center for referrals.

- Try to help children understand that sometimes things happen that are nobody's fault. "Ruth achieved this by drawing a special book for her young son, Michael. It showed a family of birds, in which the father bird was killed accidentally and the mother bird and baby bird lived in the nest alone. This became Michael's favorite book, and he would read it to his toys, explaining death to them. It was very hard, and sad, for adult relatives to hear him do this . . . but it removed all elements of guilt, allowing Michael a very early acceptance of what had happened."[2] You can find books like the one described here in your library or bookstore.

- Don't be afraid to share memories of the dead parent with the children. Remembering the parent reminds the children of the important relationship they shared and reassures them that he isn't forgotten, even if there are tears.

- Don't try to hide your grief from your children. They'll see that you're sad, and verbalizing why will help them learn to talk about and express their own feelings.

- Children may become preoccupied with thinking about Daddy. During the times the children miss Daddy most, they may say they want to go to him or die, too. That's their way of saying they want to see him again.

- Don't feel like you need to have all of the answers for your child. He or she may just need to talk without hearing much response from you. A hug or your shoulder to cry on may be more important than what you say.

- Some adults may want to conduct a special memorial service just for the children, which the children can help plan and participate in. The children could invite their friends.

- Give children the opportunity to participate in activities they enjoy. Returning them to school and their regular routines will help children feel more stable and secure.

- Be sure the children's teachers know that a parent died.

Developmental Stages of Grief

It's important to relate to children in ways appropriate to their levels of development. Following are some characteristics of grieving associated with each stage of growth:

Birth through Three Years of Age

A child's first understanding of death is his awareness of separation. Babies know things are different but don't know why. They sense emotional changes in the adults who care for them and notice when there are more people around than normal. A baby's response to death may include becoming irritable, changing eating or sleeping routines, or showing fear of strangers.

Ages Three through Six

Young children tend to think the world revolves around their experience. They can't conceive of life without their parents because they are dependent on them for daily care. Their inability to separate their existence from their parents makes the death of a parent hard to understand. Children between the ages of three and six think death is temporary, like a nap or a trip to the grocery store. They may seem to understand that their Daddy is dead, but think he'll be back later.

Because they think of death as temporary, they may not seem to be affected by it. These children will eventually realize that Daddy won't come back, and then they may need reassurance that they won't be abandoned by Mommy, too. They may be clingy and afraid to let their mother out of sight.

Once children in this age group understand that death is final, they'll think about how events relate to each other and will probably connect thoughts that don't belong together. They may think that if Daddy died in an airplane, when they get in an airplane they'll die, too. (Or if Grandma is coming to visit on an airplane, she may be in danger.) They may ask indirect questions to find out if someone else is going to die. For example, if they wonder whether they are going to die, they may ask you if they are going to go in an airplane.

Fairy tale thinking is common in young children, and they may think Daddy's death is like a magical story. To be sure your children are sorting out their thoughts and emotions realistically, if you have children between the ages of three and six you may want to consider the following concepts:

- Help them understand that they did not cause the death.
- Daddy's death is not connected to any event they experienced or thought about.
- Everyone cries when people die, and crying is OK.
- Everyone feels sad when people die, and miss the dead person. These young children know how they feel, but can't understand grief.
- Their understanding of death may be reflected in their play. It's common for young children to recreate the death in some way as they play. The playtime helps the death become more real for them.
- We'll miss Daddy a lot, but we'll be able to live without him now that we have to.
- We may not want to eat or sleep when we're supposed to. This happens because death upsets us, and after awhile we'll be OK again.
- They may regress in behaviors like thumb sucking, bed-wetting, or sleeping through the night. These are responses to the death, and will likely be temporary.
- They may become fearful. If you sense fear, ask them if they feel afraid.

Ages Six through Nine

Before children are ten-years-old they may think of death as a person, maybe a bogeyman, or ghost. To them, death comes to get you. They may think death is contagious, like the flu or a cold. They usually understand that death is final, and are ready for a short description of how their Daddy died. As you explain things to children this age, remember that they don't know that many words sound alike but have more than one meaning (for example: soul and sole).[3] Be sure they know what the words you use mean.

Children may feel embarrassed and not know how to act, so they may react in what seems to be an inappropriate manner. For example, they might act silly or become totally withdrawn. They may have trouble concentrating in school, and their schoolwork may suffer. Some children in this age group may have sleeping problems, headaches, stomachaches, or develop stuttering or nail biting. Since they usually don't know how to act when someone dies, they need adults to help them know what to say and do. You may want to talk to children ages six through nine about the following concepts:

- Be sure they understand that they did nothing to cause the death.
- Daddy's death is not going to make any of us die if we are near him.
- Everyone cries when someone dies, and that is OK.
- Everyone feels bad when someone dies.
- Encourage them to talk about their memories of life with Daddy.
- Children may be afraid or angry when someone they love dies.
- When someone dies we feel like something important is missing.
- Adults feel mixed-up, too, when someone they love dies. You may want to talk about your feelings to help the children talk about theirs.
- They may react by fantasizing about the way the death occurred and how it might have been different. In their imagination they may even think of ways they could have affected the death or changed what happened.
- Encourage the children to use communication that is different than talking to express how they feel. Maybe drawing a picture will help, or play-acting with toys. Some children might want to "play violent games in which cars crash and burn to get their feelings out."[4]

Ages Nine through Twelve

As children grow, they develop a strong sense of what is right and wrong. They'll apply this sense to areas of their lives they think it applies to, and as a result may think that Daddy's death could be a punishment for something they did. They may think that every time there is a death a baby is born, and that is related to their Dad's death. Although those ideas are not realistic, children between the ages of nine and twelve do understand what death is and that death is final. They are often conscious of the affect the death has on their lives, and may even think about how it relates to the family structure. Children in this age group may wonder how the family will be able to pay the bills and buy groceries now that Dad died. You may want to tell them, at least in a general way, how the family will be supported financially.

Children in this age group are likely to show what they feel as a response to the death, but they may not show their feelings in ways that are obvious to you. They may have trouble concentrating in school, and their schoolwork may suffer. Some children in this age group may have sleeping problems, headaches, stomachaches, or start stuttering or biting their nails. If you see any of these behaviors in your children, help them understand that they are probably responses to their father's death. Ask your children to repeat what you've said to be sure they understand. You may also want to talk to them about the following concepts:

- They weren't responsible for the death.
- We can't kill someone by wishing they would die.
- They may feel anger about the death. Anger may be a result of their strong desire to fit in with other children, but the death sets them apart as different.
- Everyone feels sad and cries when someone dies; that's OK and expected.
- They may not be sure how they should act, or become very judgmental. Reactions vary from criticism to kind sensitivity.
- Assure them that the family will have enough money to live even though Dad died, although there may be changes.

Teenagers

Teenagers understand death, although their responses are different than adults may expect. They may have adult-like responses, but at the same time may become critical, philosophic, or spend time daydreaming. Don't assume that they can handle their grief and emotion alone. They may be trying to hold it all inside to be strong for those around them. They may wonder whether Dad's death changes their roles in the family. They may feel like it's their duty to help run the family and get them through the grieving.

You may want to talk with teenagers about the following ideas:

- People often feel like they have to be strong when someone dies, so they may not want to let others know how they feel. It isn't necessary to be strong to show friends a good image. Everyone feels bad when someone dies, and many people show that by crying. Crying is OK.
- Ask your teenagers what Dad's death means for them.
- They may be nervous or complain of physical ailments. Without discounting their pain, help them understand that people often feel as they do when they face deaths in their families. Reassure them.
- We don't use drugs, alcohol, or anger to help kill our pain. If they engage in unacceptable behavior, talk to them frankly about it, asking why they did what they did, and ask them how they think you should handle it. They'll know you respect them even if you don't approve of their behavior. They may not show it, but they want you to tell them you are in control and hold them accountable to live within their boundaries. Help them find acceptable ways to respond to Dad's death.
- Expect emotions to fluctuate. Teenagers are often confused about their emotions and express their emotion in a variety of ways. "A wildly hysterical outburst may be followed by embarrassed laughter as the child tries to get a grip on himself, to act like an adult. One moment he may idealize the dead person, making him superhuman, the next moment condemn him."[5]

- Expect teenagers to look for support outside of the family rather than within it. They're likely to talk to friends, including other adults in their lives, and you shouldn't feel threatened by that.
- Their tendency to talk with others isn't an excuse to ignore their needs. Talk to them and comfort them.
- Encourage teenagers to become involved in community activities after the pain of Dad's death begins to subside. Helping others may help them regain a positive outlook and give their lives renewed purpose.
- Involvement in extra-curricular activities at school (music, art, sports, etc.) may help relieve their stress.
- They don't have responsibility for the family now. Don't let older children try to fill the gap left by the parent who died. A teenager cannot be the "man of the house" or "take over for Mom." Give them responsibilities they can handle. You may want to give them the responsibility for yard work, keeping gas in the family car, helping with cooking meals, or doing laundry. They aren't ready to assume control of the family budget or constant care of younger children.

1. Schaefer, Dan, and Christine Lyons. *How Do We Tell the Children.*: (New York, NY: Newmarket Press, 1986), 120.
2. Ibid, 211.
3. Schaefer and Lyons, 21.
4. Ibid, 92.
5. Ibid, 93.

· 8 ·

RESOURCES TO PREPARE AND HELP THOSE WHO GRIEVE

- *The Art of Condolence*
  by Leonard Zunin

- **Published by Channing L. Bete Co.:**
  Transition and the Family
  About Family Care Plans
  Protect Your Family With a Family Care Plan
  Being A Guardian For a Military Member
  Why You Should Have a Will
  Parents and Stress
  Stress and Your Child
  What You Should Know About Stress and Your Child
  MISSION: READINESS: A Personal and Family Guide

  Available from your Family Support Center, your chaplain or
  the publisher:
  > Scriptographic Booklets
  > Channing L. Bete Co. Inc.
  > 200 State Road
  > South Deerfield, MA 01373-0200
  > (800) 477-4776

e-mail: custsvcs@channing-bete.com
www.channing-bete.com

- *Today's Military Wife*
  by Lydia Sloan Cline
  Available at bookstores; published by Stackpole Books.

- *Handbook for Military Families*
  Supplement to *Army Times*, *Navy Times*, and *Air Force Times*, updated and enclosed in the *Times* in April of each year. Available in military exchanges, by subscription, or in libraries.

- **Published by Abbey Press:**
  Care Notes:
    Cherishing Your Memories of a Loved One
    Finding Your Way After the Death of a Spouse
    Finding Strength to Survive a Crisis or Tragedy
    Taking the Time You Need to Grieve Your Loss
    Getting Through the Annual Reminders of Your Loss
    Learning to Live Alone
    Helping a Child Grieve and Grow
    Planning the Funeral of Someone You Love
    Searching for God When You Lose Someone Close
    Sharing Your Grief, Easing Your Loss
    Taking Care of Yourself While Grieving
    Walking With God Through Grief and Loss
    When Grief Won't Go Away
    When Death Comes Unexpectedly to Someone You Love
    Coping in a Time of Trauma
    Letting Tears Bring Healing and Renewal
    Comforting a Friend or Loved One at the Funeral Home
    Finding Ways to Help Someone Who is Grieving
    Losing Someone Close
    Being a Friend to Someone Who Hurts

Care Notes for Teens:
> *Bad Things: Wanting to Know Why They Happen*
> *Sadness: When Life Hurts Too Much*

Prayer Notes:
> *Letting God Be With You at a Time of Loss*

Hope Notes:
> *Feeling God's Love . . . in the Midst of Suffering*
> *Finding Comfort . . . When You've Lost Someone Close*

Ask your chaplain if these titles (all published by Abbey Press) are available at your chapel or if your chapel can provide them.

Abbey Press Books:
> *Grief: How to Live with Sorrow*
> *Children Facing Grief: Letters From Bereaved Brothers and Sisters*
> *Walk on in Peace: A Thoughtful Companion for Those Who Suffer the Pain of Loss*

Self-Help Books:
> *Grief Therapy*

Abbey Consolation Books Series:
> *Finding Your Way Through Grief*
> *Grief Quest: Reflections for Men Coping With Loss*
> *A Pilgrimage Through Grief: Healing the Soul's Hurt After Loss*
> *What Helps the Most . . . When Hope is Hard to Find: 101 Insights From People Who Have Been There*
> *What Helps the Most . . . When You Lose Someone Close: 101 Insights From People Who Have Been There*

Ask your chaplain about whether these titles are available at your chapel, or contact the publisher:

> Abbey Press
> St. Meinrad, IN 47577
> (888) 374-4226
> (800) 962-4760
> www.AbbeyPress.com

• **Published by The Bureau For At-Risk Youth:**
Titles in the Family Forum Library—Military Edition:
> *Loss and Change in the Military Family*

Stress and the Military Family
Anger Management and Conflict Resolution in the Military
Communication Skills for the Military Family
Available from your Family Support Center, your chaplain or the publisher:
The Bureau For At-Risk Youth
135 Dupont Street
P.O. Box 760
Plainview, NY 11803-0760
(800) 99-YOUTH
e-mail: info@at-risk.com
www.at-risk.com

- *Single-Parent Family*
  A monthly insert to the *Focus on the Family Magazine*;
  Single-Parent Family Edition of *Focus on the Family Magazine*
  8605 Explorer Drive
  Colorado Springs, CO 80995
  (800) 424-1984

- **The Air Force Enlisted Men's Widows and Dependents Home Foundation, Inc.**
  This foundation provides homes for widows of Air Force, Air National Guard, or Air Force Reserve enlisted personnel. Although they normally accept widows only 55 or older, younger widows may be admitted.
  AF Enlisted Men's Widows and Dependents Home Found., Inc.
  92 Sunset Lane
  Shalimar, FL 32579
  (800) 258-1413
  www.afenlistedwidows.org

- **Army Emergency Relief (AER)**
  200 Stovall Street, Room 5-N-13
  Alexandria, VA 22332-0600
  (703) 428-0000
  DSN: 328-0000

online access: www.aerhq.org
e-mail: aer@aerhq.org

- **The Air Force Aid Society**
  1745 Jefferson Davis Highway, Suite 202
  Arlington, VA 22202
  (703) 607-3064
  online access: www.afas.org

- **Coast Guard Mutual Assistance**
  Commandant (G-ZMA)
  2100 2nd Street SW, Room 5502
  Washington, DC 20593-0001
  (800) 881-2462
  online access: www.cgmahq.org

- **Navy-Marine Corps Relief Society**
  801 North Randolph Street, Suite 1228
  Arlington, VA 22203-1978
  (703) 696-4904; M-F 8:15 AM–4:15 PM
  online access: www.nmcrs.org

- **Civilian Health and Medical Program of the Department of Veterans Affairs (CHAMPVA)**
  This medical benefits program helps pay for health care for surviving family members. Families must be registered with DEERS to receive CHAMPVA. For information or if you have questions about whether you are eligible, contact:
  CHAMPVA Registration Center
  P. O. Box 65023
  Denver, CO 80206-5023
  (800) 733-8387
  www.va.gov

- **Air Force Village**
  Air Force Village is a retirement complex for Air Force Officers and widows of officers. Younger widows of Air Force Officers

may also live there for a year while they decide where they may want to live. For information contact:

    Air Force Village Foundation, Inc.
    5100 John D. Ryan Blvd.
    San Antonio, TX 78245-3502
    (800) 762-1122
    www.airforcevillages.com
    Also see www.afvw.com to refer to Air Force Village West, in Riverside, CA.

- **Web sites to Consult:**

    Veterans Affairs Web Site
    www.va.gov
    Provides information about burial benefits.

    Pentagon Web Site
    www.militaryfuneralhonors.osd.mil
    Provides information about military funeral honors.

    National Cemetery System
    www.cem.va.gov

    Air Crash Support Network
    1594 York Ave, Box 22
    New York, NY 10028
    (877) ACSN-HELP
    www.aircrashsupport.com
    E-mail: info@aircrashsupport.com
    This organization aids and facilitates the grieving process of people affected by or involved in an air crash, by support, referral, and partnership of survivors and volunteers.

    Grief Recovery Online Widows and Orphans
    www.groww.org

Sena Foundation
www.sena.org
(804) 633-7575
Works with those going through catastrophic loss.

Widow Net
www.fortnet.org/widownet
Self-help resource by and for widows and widowers.

Wings of Light
www.wingsoflight.org
Non-profit support organization to support families, friends, rescue and support personnel.

SUPPORT GROUP INFORMATION

- **Tragedy Assistance Program for Survivors, Inc. (TAPS)**
  2001 S Street NW, Suite 300
  Washington, DC 20009
  (800) 959-8277
  Online access: www.taps.org
  TAPS supports surviving families and helps them pick up the pieces of their lives after a serviceman's death. They provide comfort, peer support, information and referral, assistance to military casualty officers and commanders, and hold camps for children who have lost a parent.

- **National League of Families of American Prisoners and Missing in Southeast Asia**
  Mailing address:
  1001 Connecticut Ave, NW, Suite 918
  Washington, DC 20036
  (202) 223-6846
  Web site with useful links: www.pow-miafamilies.org

- **Gold Star Wives of America**
  P.O. Box 361986
  Birmingham, AL 35236
  Toll-free (888) 751-6350
  Gold Star Wives is an organization of women whose husbands
  have died in military service. They are the widows of servicemen of all ranks, races, and creeds. The organization serves
  military widows and their dependents by offering information
  about their entitlements and understanding of the problems
  unique to the service widow.

- **Parents Without Partners**
  1650 South Dixie Highway, Suite 510
  Boca Raton, FL 33432
  (561) 391-8833
  www.parentswithoutpartners.org
  This organization is international and offers discussion groups,
  workshops, and publications. They teach practical parenting
  and help single parents learn how to be alone without being
  lonely, how to communicate more effectively, and how to enjoy life as a single parent.

- **American Self-Help Clearinghouse**
  St. Clares-Riverside Medical Center
  25 Pocono Road
  Denville, NJ 07834
  They offer a book entitled *The Self-Help Sourcebook—Finding
  and Forming Mutual Aid Self-Help Groups,* compiled by Barbara
  J. White and Edward J. Madara. The book identifies organizations that provide mutual help opportunities, and discusses
  differences between self-help and professionally run groups.
  Characteristics and dynamics of self-help groups are also dis-
  cussed. The book was published in 1992.

RESOURCES FOR HELPING CHILDREN

* *Saying Goodbye When You Don't Want To*
  Teens Dealing With Loss
  by Martha Bolton

* **Published by The Bureau For At-Risk Youth:**
  Titles from the For Parents Only Series:
  > *Dealing With Your Child's Feelings*
  > *Encouraging a Positive Attitude*
  > *Building Positive Parent/Child Communication*
  > *Teaching Your Child to Make Smart Choices*
  > *Getting Along Better With Your Child*
  > *Keeping Your Child Drug-Free*
  > *Building Your Child's Self-Esteem*
  > *Teaching Conflict Resolution Skills*
  > *Teaching Your Child Responsibility*
  > *Motivating Your Child to Success*

  Titles from the Family Forum Library:
  > *Coping With Death and Grief*

  Titles from the Need to Know Library:
  > *Grieving When a Parent Dies*

  Titles in the Kids in Crisis Video Series:
  > *How to Survive a Death in the Family*

  For Teens Only—Military Edition pamphlets:
  > *Where to Turn For Guidance and Support*
  > *Dealing With Death and Grief*

  Available from your Family Support Center, your chaplain or the publisher:
  > The Bureau For At-Risk Youth
  > 135 Dupont Street
  > P.O. Box 760
  > Plainview, NY 11803-0760
  > (800) 99-YOUTH
  > e-mail: info@at-risk.com
  > www.at-risk.com

- *Death as a Fact of Life*
  By David Hendin
  Refer to Chapter 6: Children and Death

- *How Do We Tell the Children?*
  By Dan Schaefer and Christine Lyons
  Newmarket Press, New York: 1986

V

THE TOTAL FORCE

· 1 ·

TOTAL FORCE DEPLOYMENT

When they think of the military services, many people automatically think of Active Duty forces. However, the military components are made up of more than just Active Duty forces. Today's military in the United States consists of Active Duty Army, Air Force, Navy, Marines, and Coast Guard, with Reserve components of each, as well as the Air National Guard and Army National Guard. Each component has its own mission and works to coordinate with the other components to meet the missions of the Department of Defense.

In 1969 DOD first announced the Total Force Policy. This policy views all components of the military as a single military force in which each component has equal standing. DOD draws the components together in joint training and missions to enable them to function as one total force rather than as individual components.

The equal standing of the components makes all components equally susceptible to deployment. Some people believe those in the Reserve and Guard and their families are more affected by deployment than Active Duty personnel, since Active Duty personnel already live in the military environment. Some of the needs of personnel in the Reserves and Guards are different than needs of Active Duty personnel, but neither should be minimized. Deployment disrupts life and causes pain for *all* families involved in military service. Instead of talking about who is impacted more by deployments, families need to find ways to help each other through family separations and support each other.

Families of Reservists and Guard members may find more support from the Active Duty community than they dreamed was available to them. Before you're deployed, whether you're Active Duty, Reserve, or Guard, be sure your family has someone to call when they need help. It will be most helpful if the person they call knows and understands the military system. Anything your family can do to connect with the Active Duty, Reserve, and Guard communities will make them feel less isolated or alienated when the family is separated for military reasons. Preparation for inevitable family separations helps your family appreciate the military lifestyle even during the unpleasant times.

To best understand the Total Force Policy, your family should know some general information about all of the military components, programs, and services.

"A major finding in this survey of Reservist and National Guard spouses is that they live in a civilian, rather than a military, world. Only about one-fifth reside within 25 miles of a military installation while 37% live over 100 miles from one. It is perhaps not surprising that most of these spouses have had no experience with a variety of Army Services. . . . The services with which they are familiar tend to be non-installation based: 45% have experience with CHAMPUS, 28% with the Family Assistance Center (these were established at reserve centers) and 25% with the Red Cross." [Rosenberg, 37.]

· 2 ·
THE ACTIVE DUTY COMPONENTS

The Active Duty components are the Army, Air Force, Navy, Marines, and Coast Guard. All branches of the military work hard to provide a good quality of life for service personnel and their families. Military members should be sure their families know what benefits they have and how to use them. You are welcome to use services you are entitled to on any installation. Each branch of the Active Duty force has the following services available to members and their families:

MILITARY OFFICES

Legal Assistance

Legal assistance is available at no charge to Active Duty service members and their spouses. The Legal office can draft Powers of Attorney (POA) for specific or general needs, draw up wills, and provide counseling relating to sworn statements, debts, insurance, personal property, automobiles, real estate, houses, sales and leases, taxes, estates, and claims. They can tell you what your legal rights are in specific situations, and can contact people to whom you

owe money to try to make payment arrangements with them before any legal action is taken against you. Many legal offices also
have notary service. Legal assistance can't represent you in civil or
criminal matters that fall under civilian law.

Chaplain Services

Chaplains are responsible for the spiritual, religious, moral,
and personal well being of military personnel and their families.
They offer pastoral care, religious services, Sunday school, CCD,
Bible Study groups, and family fellowship events. Chaplains are
available for counseling and are sworn to confidentiality. If you
have a specific problem that they are not able to deal with or you
want to counsel with a chaplain of your specific faith, they will
refer you to the appropriate places. Chaplains are available for
emergencies after duty hours through the Command Duty Officer.

Casualty Assistance

The Casualty Assistance Office notifies and assists family members if their active-duty sponsor dies or becomes unaccounted for.
They provide guidance and counseling relating to survivor benefits, arrange for travel, and provide immediate assistance to next-
of-kin.

Inspector General (IG)

One of the purposes of the IG is to be available for service
members and their families to help to resolve problems related to
the military if the chain of command can't solve the problems.

Family Services

Each branch of the military has a Family Services organization
to help meet the needs of personnel and their families. The Army
has Army Community Service Centers (ACS). The Air Force has
Family Support Centers (FSC). The Navy and Marine Corps have
Family Service Centers (FSC). The Coast Guard has Work-Life
Centers. The Family Service Centers in all branches of the military

offer parallel services that may include the following: job search assistance; information and referral; informational meetings and counseling for budgeting, investments, credit management, and personal financial planning; opportunities to do volunteer work; relocation assistance; a 24-hour hotline; transition assistance for those leaving Active Duty; career workshops; resume workshops; and individual counseling.

Family Services Programs help people in transition, have information about other military installations, and operate loan closets where you can borrow household items while you're between moves. The centers are also able to refer you to other organizations.

The Military Assistance Program Site, MAPsite, is a 24-hour cybercenter run by the Family Policy Office at the Defense Department to support military families around the world. The MAPsite enhances the military family centers, and can be accessed at the following address: http://dticaw.dtic.mil/mapsite.

Finance and Accounting

The Finance office can help you set up automatic allotments from your regular pay and answer all pay-related questions. If there is a special pay to which you are entitled because of deployment (such as hazardous duty pay or family separation pay) talk to them about it.

Housing

Housing helps military families find acceptable housing either in government quarters or in the civilian community. If you have housing problems, they can advise you.

Military Police/Shore Police/Security Force

The Military Police, Shore Police, and Security Force are the military installation police departments.

Transportation

The Transportation Management Office (TMO) coordinates your moves as well as other official travel-related issues, including movement of household goods and automobiles.

SATO (Scheduled Airline Ticket Office)

SATO works in cooperation with the Transportation office to arrange moves that require airline tickets and other official travel. Many installations have a branch of SATO that can be used by family members to arrange personal travel.

Recreation Services

Recreation services offer activities and entertainment for both single military members and families. Some of the services they may have available are the following: Information, Tickets, and Travel Office (ITT), with information and tickets for tourist attractions, cultural events, and sports events, often at a discount; theaters; picnic parks; softball fields, volleyball and horseshoe areas; hobby, sewing, and craft classes; ceramic and pottery studios; wood shops; picture framing; photo labs; auto hobby shops; retail stores to support hobbies; bowling; golf; camping and rental of outdoor equipment.

Health Care

The government has a medical program to supply health care for military members and their families. Complete medical and dental care is provided for the Active Duty member. Medical and dental care are provided to family members by the military medical treatment facilities and supplemented by civilian care when necessary.

DEERS

The Defense Enrollment Eligibility Reporting System (DEERS) verifies that individuals are eligible to receive military health benefits. Active Duty members are automatically enrolled in DEERS, but they must register family members at the installation personnel office. Family members cannot receive medical care at government expense or use CHAMPUS or TRICARE unless they are enrolled in DEERS. If you have questions about DEERS, ask at your military personnel center.

CHAMPUS (Civilian Health and Medical Program of the Uniformed Services)

CHAMPUS is a benefit for dependents of service members to help with medical care if it isn't available at the local military facility or in an emergency when the closest hospital is not military. You pay a deductible and a small percentage of the bill and CHAMPUS pays the rest. See the TRICARE information below for more details. (You can also ask the Health Benefits Advisor at the military clinic or hospital nearest you for information.)

TRICARE

TRICARE is a health care program that expands CHAMPUS coverage. TRICARE addresses the increasing need for military families to receive care from civilian providers when military medical treatment facilities can't meet their needs. TRICARE offers a choice of health care plans. TRICARE is now the comprehensive health care plan for the military; what was known as CHAMPUS is now called TRICARE Standard, which is one of the options within TRICARE. Ask the Health Benefits Advisor in the TRICARE or CHAMPUS office of the military medical treatment facility nearest you for more information. If you don't live near an installation, you can find information about TRICARE at your unit.

PRIMUS and NAVCARE

In some areas there are satellite medical care clinics located off of the military installation. They have been called PRIMUS (Primary Care for the Uniformed Services) and NAVCARE centers in the past. In the TRICARE plan they are called TRICARE outpatient clinics.

TRICARE Active Duty Family Member Dental Plan

The TRICARE Active Duty Family Member Dental Plan is the DOD dental insurance plan offered to families of Active Duty personnel. You pay a small monthly fee and receive care from civilian dentists. The Health Benefits Advisor at your TRICARE or

CHAMPUS office can give you details about the dental plan and answer your questions.

Liaison Offices

Each branch of the military has a liaison office to serve family members. Here are the addresses and phone numbers of those offices:

Army: HQDA
Army Family Liaison Office
Room 2D653, The Pentagon
Washington, DC 20310-0300
(703) 695-7714 (in Virginia)
(800) 833-6622
E-mail: dgwfo@aol.com
or: whited@Pentagon-braco.army.mil
www.aflo.org

Air Force: Air Force Family Matters Office
HQ USAF/DPPH
The Pentagon
Washington, DC 20330-5060
(703) 697-4720
www.afcrossroads.com

Navy: Navy Family Support Office
The Naval Services FamilyLine
Washington Navy Yard, Building 172
1254 - 9th Street SE, Suite 104
Washington, DC 20374-5067
DSN: 288-2333
Commercial: (202) 433-2333
Office hours: M-F, 10 AM–1 PM EST/EDT
www.lifelines2000.org/familyline

Marine Corps:Marine Corps Family Programs Branch
            Marine Corps Family Team Building
            MCCS HQ USMC
            Manpower and Reserve Affairs
            3280 Russell Road
            Quantico, VA 22134-5103
            e-mail: mcftb@manpower.usmc.mil
            www.usmc-mccs.org/MCFTB

Coast Guard: U. S. Coast Guard Family Programs
            Commandant (G-WKW)
            Office of Work Life
            USCG HQ Room 6320
            2100 2nd Street SW
            Washington, DC 20593-0001
            (202) 267-6160 or 267-6263

PRIVATE ORGANIZATIONS

Relief Societies

The Army Emergency Relief, Air Force Aid Society, Navy-Marine Corps Relief Society, and Coast Guard Mutual Assistance are parallel charity organizations to help service members and their families with financial emergencies. Policies vary between them, but they all work in much the same way. The Relief Societies are usually located in Family Service Centers on military installations. They don't charge for their services and rely on donations for funding. They usually offer help in the form of interest-free loans or grants for basic needs such as rent, utility bills, food, travel for a funeral, moving, or car repair. They consider any valid request for emergency financial help. The Aid Societies also offer Guaranteed Parent Loans and other forms of tuition assistance, budgeting advice, and assistance to families when a military member dies. Information about the relief societies can be found online at www.famnet.com under emergency financial assistance.

Red Cross

The Red Cross is available 24-hours a day. Most people know they are there to help during disasters or death notification, but they offer much more than that. The services they have available may include communication to help with requests for Emergency Leave; financial assistance for food, clothing, shelter, and transportation to help you through unexpected financial emergencies; swimming lessons; lifeguard instruction; CPR classes and certification; babysitting classes; opportunities to volunteer your time to help others; and their worldwide communication network will send a message to request information on the health and welfare of a family member if it's been more than three weeks since you've heard from him and you're concerned that everything is all right (this is a drastic and last resort step to take, since the commander and chaplain will then become involved).

Wives Clubs/Spouse Clubs

Wives or spouse clubs exist on most military installations. There are usually separate clubs for wives/spouses of officers and wives/spouses of enlisted members. They provide a social environment to help wives/spouses make friends and are involved in charitable projects. Most of the members are wives, although husbands may and do join these clubs.

USO (United Service Organization)

The USO runs airport centers, Navy fleet centers, and community centers to help military members and their families adjust to unfamiliar surroundings. They provide tours, activities, and discount tickets for local events. They also encourage Americans stationed overseas to participate in events of their host nation.

Armed Services YMCA

Armed Services YMCAs try to provide recreational services needed at military installations to supplement what the installation offers. They do not charge fees but a valid ID card is required. To learn more about them, access their Web site at: www.asymca.org

· 3 ·
The Guard and Reserve
Components

There are three general categories of personnel in the Reserves. The Ready Reserve consists of military members in the Reserve and National Guard that are available to be called to Active Duty to augment the Active Duty components during a war or national emergency. The Standby Reserve includes personnel who don't perform drills in units, but could be involuntarily called to Active Duty during a war or national emergency. Standby Reserves aren't mobilized unless there aren't enough members available in the Ready Reserve. The Retired Reserve is made up of personnel who receive retirement pay because of their military service. The personnel in Retired Reserve aren't normally eligible to be ordered to Active Duty.

The Ready Reserve can be activated in three ways: volunteerism, presidential call-up, and mobilization. Volunteerism allows a member to be placed on Active Duty with his consent. The President may order selected Guard or Reserve members to Active Duty to augment the Active Duty forces for specific missions or for national emergencies. Mobilization brings Ready Reserve units and individual members to Active Duty in times of war or national emergency. Each Reserve and Guard unit has its own mission.

The National Guard includes the Army National Guard (ARNG) and Air National Guard (ANG). They augment the Active Duty military and meet state and local needs relating to natural disasters and civil uprisings. The National Guard Bureau works to develop and maintain Army and Air Guard units. The Bureau also acts as a liaison between individual states and the Departments of the Army and Air Force.

The Reserve Component of the Army is the largest Reserve Component. The Reserve Component of the Air Force includes the Air Force Reserve. The Naval Reserve is the Reserve Component of the Navy, and the Marine Corps Reserve is the Reserve Component of the Marine Corps. In addition to these Reserve Components, there are the Fleet Reserves. When enlisted Navy or Marine Corps members retire from Active Duty after twenty or more years, they are automatically transferred to the Fleet Reserve. Members of either Fleet Reserve component are eligible to be involuntarily recalled to Active Duty or called to active training until they complete thirty years of service, when they are transferred out of the Fleet Reserves. The Coast Guard also has a Reserve Component.

Reservists, like Active Duty personnel, are entitled to military benefits because of their military service. While serving on Active Duty, or drill, they are normally entitled to the following benefits: Serviceman's Group Life Insurance, the use of military exchanges, limited use of military commissaries, medical care for injuries connected with their duty, access to military clothing stores, access to military dining facilities, access to military theaters, space-available access to military billeting, space-available access to air transportation within the United States, and certain survivor benefits.[1]

1. Hunter, Ronald S., MSG Gary L. Smith, USA (Retired), and Debra M. Gordon, editors. *1996 Reserve Forces Almanac*. (Falls Church, VA: Reserve Forces Almanac, 1996), 63.

· 4 ·

WILL YOU BE READY?

I hope military families of all components prepare themselves for deployments and military separations so that when they face separations they'll be equipped to cope with them. Now more military personnel than ever are called on to take a turn, or a second or third turn, on deployments that separate them from their families. Tech. Sgt. Michael Gilbertson spoke for many military members and their families when he said that every successive deployment becomes more difficult.[1]

My husband was deployed on only two hours' notice. We had no idea he would be sent because another chaplain was designated as the mobility chaplain. When crises occur, however, all rules and predictability are subject to change. I was blessed because we were stationed at a base where there was a wonderful support program set up for families within the first weeks of the deployment. Weekly meetings continued until everyone returned home and the regular three-month replacement rotations were begun.

The meetings provided me a sense of connection with my husband because they brought the most recent information to us, and a sense of connection to other deployed spouses I met at the meetings and formed friendships with. My husband said he felt good knowing that the base was taking good care of us.

My friend, who was stationed at another base, went through the deployment of her husband with no base support. Not all families have supportive environments during separations. However most installations are prepared to help the families left behind. I hope this book helps you prepare for deployment or military separation, so you know where to look for help when it's your turn. If you're at an installation that doesn't provide a supportive environment, you may be able to bring ideas to key people who can begin a family support program. You'll be happy you did!

1. Author unknown, "It never gets any easier to leave." *Air Force Times*, 27 October 1997: 11.

· 5 ·
RESOURCES FOR ALL COMPONENTS OF THE MILITARY

RESOURCES FOR SINGLE MILITARY MEMBERS

- **Published by The Bureau For At-Risk Youth:**
  From the Family Forum Library—Military Edition:
  Single in the Military
  Anger Management and Conflict Resolution in the Military
  The Single Military Parent
  Available from your chaplain or the publisher:
  The Bureau For At-Risk Youth
  135 Dupont Street
  P.O. Box 760
  Plainview, NY 11803-0760
  (800) 99-YOUTH
  e-mail: info@at-risk.com
  www.at-risk.com

Resources for All Military Personnel and Their Families

- **INTERNET**
  There are many Web sites offering support for military families. A good place to start looking for military family information is on the **World Wide Web Military Pages-Group Family,** at: www.militarydataresource.com/group_family.htm
  Other web sites of interest may be:

  Military Wives
  www.militarywives.com
  www.marinewives.com
  www.navywives.com
  www.armywives.com
  www.airforcewives.com
  www.militarywivesandmoms.org

  Military Spouse Support Network
  members.aol.com/widowclub/index.html
  Support for spouses during deployments or family separations. Connects spouses who are going through family separation, offers a chat room, and personal Web pages.

  These sites provide peer support for spouses of all branches:
  www.spousenet.com
  www.militaryfamily.com
  www.CincHouse.com (short for Commander-in-Chief of the House; includes an on-line chat room and resources for military women and spouses)

  Sgt. Mom's
  www.sgtmoms.com
  Provides links to all branches, and covers a variety of military issues.

www.militarycity.com
This site gives military news and related information from the Military Times Publishing Group.

- *Today's Military Wife: Meeting the Challenges of Service Life*
By Lydia Sloan Cline
Available at bookstores; published by Stackpole Books.

- *Heroes at Home: Help & Hope For America's Military Families*
by Ellie Kay

- **Web Sites Operated by the National Institute for Building Long Distance Relationships.**
All of these web sites have great links, ideas, and information.

  www.daads.com
  Dads at a Distance—helps fathers who are away from their children maintain and strengthen their relationships during their absence.

  www.momsovermiles.com
  Moms Over Miles—helps mothers who have to be away to maintain and strengthen the relationships they have with their children while they're gone.

  www.longdistancecouples.com
  Long Distance Couples—helps couples maintain relationships with each other when they're separated.

  www.longdistancegrandparenting.com
  Grandparenting From a Distance

- *Uniformed Services Almanac*
Annual Editions
Ronald S. Hunter, MSG Gary L. Smith, USA (Ret), and Debra M. Gordon, Editors

Published by:
Uniformed Services Almanac, Inc.
P. O. Box 4144
Falls Church, VA 22044
(703) 532-1631
toll-free: (888) 872-9698
Fax: (703) 532-1635
e-mail: MILITARYALMANAC@MSN.COM
www.militaryalmanac.com

- **Mothers of Preschoolers (MOPS)**
MOPS International
2370 South Trenton Way
Denver, CO 80231
(303) 733-5353
Fax: (303) 733-5770
www.gospelcom.net/mops
Mops is an organization that offers support to mothers with small children. They usually meet twice a month, offering a morning of relaxing support, discussion about marriage and parenting, crafts, and friendship to young mothers while their children are cared for in age-appropriate classes where they play games, sing, listen to stories, and have a craft time. To find out if there is a MOPS group in your area consult the phone book, ask at your chapel or church, or contact the international headquarters above.

- **Military Child Education Coalition**
108 East FM 2410, Suite D
P.O. Box 2519
Harker Heights, TX 76548-2519
(254) 953-1923
www.MilitaryChild.org

- **TCKworld.com**
  This is a wonderful web site dedicated to supporting Third Culture Kids (TCKs), including military brats and others who grow up in a variety of cultures. It has lots of resources for adults and children. Check out the story of Mr. Roundhead and the rest of this site!

- **Families in Global Transition**
  www.figt.org
  Addresses challenges of global moving and living outside the continental United States. Has some good resources for moving with children.

- **Published by Channing L. Bete Co.:**
  Military Family Life
  Military Families Are Special; a coloring and activities book
  About Being Married in the Military
  Living in a Military Family
  Transition and the Family
  About Family Care Plans
  Protect Your Family With a Family Care Plan
  Family Budgeting
  Checking Accounts
  Good Money Management for Military Personnel
  Credit Management for Military Personnel
  Beat the High Cost of Living
  Why You Should Have a Will
  About Military Sponsorship
  MISSION READINESS: A Personal and Family Guide
  Available from your Family Support Center, your chaplain, or the publisher:
  Scriptographic Booklets
  Channing L. Bete Co. Inc.
  200 State Road
  South Deerfield, MA 01373-0200
  (800) 477-4776

e-mail: custsvcs@channing-bete.com
www.channing-bete.com

- **Published by The Bureau For At-Risk Youth:**
  Titles in the Family Forum Library—Military Edition:
    How to be a Successful Young Military Family
    Communication Skills for the Military Family
    The Military Lifestyle and Children
    Effective Child Discipline for Successful Military Families
    Successfully Parenting Your Adolescent in the Military
    Parenting Your Young Children in the Military
    The Single Military Parent
    Helping Children Cope With Change
    Family Readiness
  Coloring Books:
    I'm Proud to be a Military Kid
    I'll Miss You
    Welcome Home!
  For Teens Only—Military Edition:
    It's Time to Move Again
    Making the Most of the Military Lifestyle
    Adjusting to Your New School
    Appreciating Diversity in the Military
    Challenges of Living in a Single-Parent Family
  Available from your Family Support Center, your chaplain, or
  the publisher:
    The Bureau For At-Risk Youth
    135 Dupont Street
    P.O. Box 760
    Plainview, NY 11803-0760
    (800) 99-YOUTH
    e-mail: info@at-risk.com
    www.at-risk.com

- "The Military Father: Good Servicemen Can be Good Daddies too"
  By F. Sitler
  The Navy Times Magazine, February 1, 1982, pages 28–30.
  Available in many libraries.

- *Handbook for Military Families*
  Supplement to *Army Times, Navy Times,* and *Air Force Times,*
  updated and enclosed in the *Times* annually in April.
  Available by subscription, in military exchanges, and in libraries.

- **Armed Forces Hostess Association (AFHA)**
  Maintains files on facilities at military installations of all services throughout the world. www.army.mil/afha
  Write: Armed Forces Hostess Association
          Pentagon Room 1D110
          Washington, DC 20310
  Call: (703) 697-3180
          DSN: 227-6857

- **USO**
  USO World Headquarters
  1008 Eberle Place SE, Suite 301
  Washington Navy Yard, DC 20374-5096
  (202) 610-5700
  online: www.uso.org

- **National Military Family Association**
  6000 Stephenson Ave., Suite 304
  Alexandria, VA 22304-3526
  (703) 931-6632
  www.nmfa.org

- **Military Family Resource Center**
  Military Family Resource Center
  CS4, Suite 302, Room 309
  1745 Jefferson Davis Highway
  Arlington, VA 22202-3424
  phone: Commercial: (703) 602-4964
          DSN: 332-4964
  Web site: www.mfrc.calib.com
  The Military Family Resource Center is an invaluable tool for
  helping military families. They have a wide variety of Web sites
  and programs to provide help, referral and information. The
  Web sites they run include *Military Children and Youth, Military family Week, Parenting Initiatives, Child Abuse Prevention*,
  and many more special issues. Visit their Web sites to research
  how they address topics of interest to you or your organization. To contact an Information Specialist regarding any of their
  services write or call:
      Military Family Resource Center
      4040 North Fairfax Drive, Room 420
      Arlington, VA 22203-1635
      phone: DSN: 426-9053
      Commercial: (703) 696-9053
  fax: DSN: 426-9062
      Commercial: (703) 696-9062
  e-mail: mfrc@hq.odedodea.edu

- **American Red Cross**
  Military/Social Services
  National Headquarters
  17th and D Street NW
  Washington, DC 20006
  (202) 737-8300
  www.redcross.org

- **Armed Forces Services Corporation**
  2800 Shirlington Road, Suite 350
  Arlington, VA 22206-3601

Toll-free: (888) 237-2872
Local: (703) 379-9311
www.afsc-usa.com

Army Resources

- **Soldier/Family Assistance**
  Addresses issues that affect the duty environment of soldiers and civilians, and living conditions of soldiers and their families. Sponsors a Family Life Communication Line (FLCL) to family members located anywhere in the United States.
  Ask your Army Community Services for more information.

- **Army Family Liaison Office**
  DAIM-ZAF
  Room 2D665
  Assistant Chief of Staff for Installation Management
  600 Army Pentagon
  Washington, DC 20310-0600
  (703) 695-7714 (in Virginia)
  (800) 833-6622
  Autovan 225-7714
  e-mail: dgwfo@aol.com
  or: whited@Pentagon-braco.army.mil
  www.aflo.org

- **Army Emergency Relief (AER)**
  Room 5-N-13
  200 Stovall St.
  Alexandria, VA 22332-0600
  (703) 428-0000
  DSN: 328-0000
  Online: www.aerhq.org
  e-mail: aer@aerhq.org

- **Army Family Assistance Hotline**
  Fax: (800) 542-9254

- **Association of the United States Army**
  P.O. Box 1560
  2425 Wilson Boulevard
  Arlington, VA 22201
  (703) 841-4300
  (800) 336-4570
  For family programs ask for extension 150 or 151.
  www.ausa.org

- *Welcome to Your Army Community Service Center*
  Published by The Bureau For At-Risk Youth; ask for it at your
  ACS.

- **Army Community and Family Support Center Homepage**
  Online: www.armymwr.com

- *Army Community Service—For Help When You Need It*
  Available from your Family Service Center, your chaplain, or
  the publisher:
  Scriptographic Booklets
  Channing L. Bete Co. Inc.
  200 State Road
  South Deerfield, MA 01373-0200
  (800) 477-4776
  e-mail: custsvcs@channing-bete.com
  www.channing-bete.com

Air Force Resources

- *Balancing Work & Life in the U. S. Air Force*
  (includes helpful checklists and forms)

Available from your Family Support Center.

- *Welcome to Your Air Force Family Support Center*
  Published by The Bureau For At-Risk Youth; ask for it at your
  FSC.

- **Air Force Family Matters Office**
  HQ USAF/DPPH
  The Pentagon
  Washington, DC 20330-5060
  (703) 697-4720

- **Air Force Aid Society**
  Suite 202
  1745 Jefferson Davis Highway
  Arlington, VA 22202
  (703) 607-3064
  www.afas.org
  Air Force Aid offers help for families with financial emergencies, usually in the form of interest-free loans or grants for basic needs such as rent, utility bills, food, travel for a funeral,
  moving or car repair. They will consider any valid request for
  emergency financial help. The Air Force Aid Society also offers
  Guaranteed Parent Loans and other forms of tuition assistance.

- **Family Advocacy Program**
  This program was created to deal with the prevention, identification, evaluation, treatment, reporting and follow-up of child
  and spouse abuse and neglect, sexual assault, and rape. They
  conduct parent education and provide crisis intervention, treatment, and follow-up.

- **Key Spouses**
  The Air Force is also beginning a Key Spouse program. Like
  the Marine Key Volunteer Network, Key Spouses will be vol-

unteers available to help families when they need assistance. Your Family Support Center will know whether there are Key Spouses available at your base.

- **Ombudsmen**
  The Air Force has a new ombudsman program to help families with deployments. Like the Navy ombudsmen, those in the Air Force are not there to solve problems, but to help families find resources as a liaison between the families and command. To find out if there is an ombudsman on your base, contact your Family Support Center.

- **Family Readiness NCO**
  The Air Force has appointed and trained Active Duty NCOs to work at the Family Support Centers to meet the needs of families of deployed personnel. They coordinate with other caregivers on bases to hold support group meetings and help ease the stress of separation. They are effective advocates for families, and some have videophones available for families to use to keep in touch with the deployed members. Contact your Family Support Center to see what resources are available on your base.

- **Air Force WEB Page**
  The Air Force has a WEB page called Crossroads: AFCROSSROADS.COM
  This site will give you information about all DOD installations, and also has an Air Force Spouse Forum. The Forum is designed specifically for spouses to provide communication on a variety of Air Force issues, and to assist them during times of military duty that results in family separation. Spouses can post messages and participate in the following manner:
  Within the Crossroads site, click on the category entitled "Spouse Network."
  Register as a new user, creating your own user name and password.

You will receive an e-mail verifying your approval (usually within about 5 minutes).
Once approved, you can sign in and access the Spouse Forum.

Don't be worried about having to provide your Social Security Number, full name, birth date, and personal e-mail address to access sections of this WEB site. The information is verified through the DEERS records to ensure each user is authorized, and is submitted using Secure Socket Layer (SSL) encryption in order to provide the best security available and honor the privacy act. Remember that if DEERS does not have correct information, you will be denied access to the password-protected sections of Crossroads. You may want to check to be sure your DEERS records are accurate.

NAVY RESOURCES

- *Navy Family Lifeline*
  Navy Family Lifeline is a quarterly newspaper for Navy and Marine Corps spouses and dependents. It is available through the Navy Wifeline Association.

- *Sea Legs*
  Sea Legs is a handbook for Navy spouses. It is available through the Navy Wifeline Association.

- *Social Customs and Traditions of the Sea Services*
  This booklet is written by and published by the Navy Wifeline Association.

- **Naval Services FamilyLine/LIFELines Network**
  Naval Services FamilyLine was formerly known as The Navy Wifeline Association. For more information write:
      The Naval Services FamilyLine

Washington Navy Yard, Building 172
1254 - 9th Street SE, Suite 104
Washington DC 20374-5067
Phone: DSN 288-2333
        Commercial (202) 433-2333
Office hours: M–F 10AM–1PM EST/EDT
www.lifelines2000.org/familyline

- **Web Sites, such as:**
www.navymoms.org
www.navywives.com

- **Navy Mutual Aid Association**
Henderson Hall
29 Carpenter Road
Arlington, VA 22212
(800) 628-6011
Online: www.navymutual.org

- **Navy-Marine Corps Relief Society**
801 North Randolph Street, Suite 1228
Arlington, VA 22203-1978
(703) 696-4904
www.nmcrs.org

- *Welcome to Your Navy/Marine Corps Family Service Center*
Published by The Bureau For At-Risk Youth; ask for it at your
FSC.

- *Your Navy Family Service Center*
Available from your Family Service Center, your chaplain or
the publisher:
     Scriptographic Booklets
     Channing L. Bete Co. Inc.
     200 State Road
     South Deerfield, MA 01373-0200
     (800) 477-4776

e-mail: custsvcs@channing-bete.com
www.channing-bete.com

- **Ombudsman**
  The ombudsman, a volunteer, is an official representative of Navy families and works to establish and maintain good communication between the Command and the families of personnel. As a liaison for community resources, the ombudsman works to find ways to help families use the programs and services available to them, and guides shy or reluctant people to the service or agency they need. The ombudsman communicates care from the Command to the individual, but is not there to address problems between the military sponsor and the command or fill the role of a professional counselor.

- **Navy Relief Society**
  The Navy Relief Society helps meet basic living needs such as rent, utilities, and food in times of emergency. They can lend money for emergency leave travel for either spouse's immediate family or grandparents if you have a Red Cross message or verification from a doctor that requests your presence. They may be able to help you with a loan for emergency repairs if your car breaks down. The Navy Relief Society also handles Guaranteed Student Loans, and may have an emergency food pantry and thrift shop.

- **Navy Family Advocacy Program**
  The Navy Family Advocacy Program was created to deal with the prevention, identification, evaluation, treatment, reporting and follow-up of child and spouse abuse and neglect, sexual assault, and rape. They conduct parent education and provide crisis intervention, treatment, and follow-up.

- **The Chaplains Religious Development Operation (CREDO)**
  CREDO, which means, "I believe" in Latin, is a CNO (Chief of Naval Operations)-sponsored program that is conducted by

chaplains. CREDO addresses issues such as personal growth, parenting, stress management, and marriage enrichment. The foundational program they offer is a seventy-two-hour Personal Growth Retreat. It is an opportunity for individuals to pursue personal and spiritual growth in a residential setting. The major aims of the retreat are to provide participants the opportunity to develop new perspectives in their relationships with God, family, friends, shipmates, the Navy, and the broader world in which they live. Each person is encouraged to explore the basis of his or her inner spiritual resources.

MARINE CORPS RESOURCES

- **Internet For Marine Wives**
  There are Web sites specifically for Marine Corps wives, such as:
  www.marinewives.com
  www.marinemoms.online.virtualave.net

- **Key Volunteer Network (KVN)**
  The KVN is the official Marine Corps family support and communication network within a command. Key Wives assist incoming Marines and their families and make them aware of the services available to them. They also support families when sponsors are separated from their families. This program is similar to the ombudsman program in the Navy and Coast Guard.

- **Marine Corps Family Team Building (MCFTB)**
  MCCS HQ USMC
  Manpower and Reserves Affairs
  3280 Russell Road
  Quantico, VA 22134-5103
  e-mail: mcftb@manpower.usmc.mil
  www.usmc-mccs.org/MCFTB

MCFTB provides educational resources, services, and enhances the readiness of Marine Corps families. It offers a variety of helpful programs, such as PREP, CREDO, and L.I.N.K.S. Check out the web site for details.

- **Marine Corps Community Liaison Office**
  (800) USMC-CLO
  (800) 876-2256
  e-mail: PMILLS455@aol.com
  or: Mrs.PriscillaMills@MH@HQMC

- **Navy-Marine Corps Relief Society**
  801 North Randolph Street, Suite 1228
  Arlington, VA 22203-1978
  (703) 696-4904
  www.nmcrs.org
  M–F 8:15 AM–4:15 PM

- *Welcome to Your Navy/Marine Corps Family Service Center*
  Published by The Bureau For At-Risk Youth; ask for it at your FSC.

- **Marine Corps Association**
  715 Broadway Street
  MCCDC
  Quantico, VA 22134
  (703) 640-6161
  (800) 336-0291
  www.mca-marines.org

- *Your Marine Corps Family Service Center*
  Available from your Family Service Center, your chaplain, or the publisher:
  Scriptographic Booklets
  Channing L. Bete Co. Inc.
  200 State Road
  South Deerfield, MA 01373-0200

(800) 477-4776
e-mail: custsvcs@channing-bete.com
www.channing-bete.com

COAST GUARD RESOURCES

- **U. S. Coast Guard Family Programs**
Commandant (G-WKW)
Office of Work Life
2100 2nd Street SW, USCG HQ Room 6320
Washington, DC 20593-0001
(202) 267-6160 or 267-6263
Obtain the services of or information about the Work Life Program by contacting the EAPC specialist at your regional Work Life Staff. Regional staffs are located at each Integrated Support Command (ISC) in the Coast Guard.
To contact the Work Life Staff nearest you, call 1-800-872-4957, followed by the extension of the appropriate ISC location:
>Alameda, ext. 252
>Boston, ext. 301
>Cleveland, ext. 309
>Honolulu, ext. 314
>Ketchikan, ext. 317
>Kodiak, ext. 563
>Miami, ext. 307
>New Orleans, ext. 308
>Portsmouth, ext. 305
>San Pedro, ext. 311
>St. Louis, ext. 302
>Washington DC, ext. 932.

- **Ombudsman**
The ombudsman, a volunteer, is an official representative of Coast Guard families and works to establish and maintain good communication between the Command and the families of

personnel. As a liaison for community resources, the ombudsman works to find ways to help families use the programs and services available to them, and guides shy or reluctant people to the service or agency they need. The ombudsman communicates care from the Command to the individual, but is not there to address problems between the military sponsor and the command or fill the role of a professional counselor.

- **The Coast Guard Employee Assistance Program**
  Available 24 hours: 1-800-222-0364
  Callers can request help through a counselor outside the military system, and most information is kept confidential.

- **Coast Guard Chief Petty Officers Association**
  Coast Guard Enlisted Association
  5520 G Hempstead Way
  Springfield, VA 22151
  (703) 941-0395
  www.cgea.coastguard.org

- **Chief Warrant Officers Association, USCG**
  200 V Street SW
  Washington, DC 20024
  (202) 554-7753

- **Coast Guard Mutual Assistance**
  Commandant (G-ZMA)
  2100 2nd Street SW, Room 5502
  Washington, DC 20593-0001
  www.cgmahq.org
  (800) 881-2462; M–F 7 AM–4 PM Eastern

RESOURCES FOR RESERVE AND GUARD PERSONNEL AND THEIR FAMILIES

- **Guide to Reserve Family Member Benefits**
  Booklet available from the Family Support Offices
  or on the Reserve Affairs home page:
  http://raweb.osd.mil/publications/index.htm

- *National Guard Almanac*
  Reserve Forces Almanac
  Annual Editions
  Ronald S. Hunter, MSG Gary L. Smith, USA (Ret), and Debra
  M. Gordon, Editors
  Published by:
  Uniformed Services Almanac, Inc.
  P. O. Box 4144
  Falls Church, VA 22044
  (703) 532-1631
  toll-free: (888) 872-9698
  Fax: (703) 532-1635
  e-mail address: MILITARYALMANAC@MSN.COM
  www.militaryalmanac.com

- **Published by Channing L. Bete Co.:**
  About Military Family Life
  Annual Training
  You Belong to the National Guard Family
  You're Part of the National Guard Family
  You Belong to the U. S. Army Reserve Family
  About Preparing for Mobilization
  Military Families Are Special; a coloring and activities book
  Transition and the Family
  Living in a Military Family
  Making a Successful Transition

Available from your Family Support Center, your chaplain, or
the publisher:
Scriptographic Booklets
Channing L. Bete Co. Inc.
200 State Road
South Deerfield, MA 01373-0200
(800) 477-4776
e-mail: custsvcs@channing-bete.com
www.channing-bete.com

ARMY RESERVE RESOURCES

- **Family Readiness Online**
The Army Reserve offers family support programs to help families prepare for deployments. Many of these programs are
courses that are part of the Army Family Team Building Program. Operation Ready is also available to specifically address
readiness for families. To access information online, look at:
trol.redstone.army.mil/acslink

- *You Belong to the U. S. Army Reserve Family*
Available from your Family Support Center, your chaplain, or
the publisher:
Scriptographic Booklets
Channing L. Bete Co. Inc.
200 State Road
South Deerfield, MA 01373-0200
(800) 477-4776
e-mail: custsvcs@channing-bete.com
www.channing-bete.com

- **Army Reserve Association**
P.O. Box 711
Winfield, KS 67156
(800) ARMY-RES
www.armyreserve.org

- Army Reserve Headquarters Hotline
(800) 359-8483 ext. 464-8995/8947

AIR FORCE RESERVE RESOURCES

- Air Reserve Headquarters Hotline
(800) 223-1784 ext 71294

NAVAL, COAST GUARD AND MARINE CORPS
RESERVE RESOURCES

- **Ombudsman**
The Naval Reserve ombudsmen are appointed by unit commanders to help meet family needs. Many of these volunteers are married to Reservists, and have a first-hand understanding of family separation. If you don't know how to reach your ombudsman, call the human resources program manager for ombudsmen at (800) 621-8853.

The Marine Corps Reserves have liaisons in their training centers to help families, as well as key volunteers, who are comparable to Navy ombudsmen.

The Coast Guard Reserve Work Life Program supports family members. Ombudsmen are assigned to be liaisons with the Work Life Program staffs. To contact the Work Life Staff nearest you, call 1-800-872-4957, followed by the extension of the appropriate ISC location:

        Alameda, ext. 252
        Boston, ext. 301
        Cleveland, ext. 309
        Honolulu, ext. 314
        Ketchikan, ext. 317

Kodiak, ext. 563
Miami, ext. 307
New Orleans, ext. 308
Portsmouth, ext. 305
San Pedro, ext. 311
St. Louis, ext. 302
Washington DC, ext. 932.

- **Naval Reserve Association**
  1619 King Street
  Alexandria, VA 22314-2793
  (703) 548-5800
  Fax: (703) 683-3647
  e-mail: admin@navy-reserve.org
  www.navy-reserve.org

- **Marine Corps Reserve Officer's Association**
  337 Potomac Avenue
  Quantico, VA 22134
  (703) 630-3772
  Fax: (703) 630-1904
  e-mail: mcroaexdin@aol.com
  www.mcroa.com

- **Naval Enlisted Reserve Association**
  6703 Farragut Avenue
  Falls Church, VA 22042-2189
  (800) 776-9020
  www.nera.org

- **Coast Guard Reserve Web Site**
  www.uscg.mil
  click on Reserve

- **Fleet Reserve Association**
  125 N. West Street
  Alexandria, VA 22314-2754
  (703) 683-1400
  www.fra.org

NATIONAL GUARD RESOURCES

- **Enlisted Association of the National Guard of the United States**
  3133 Mt. Vernon Ave
  Alexandria, VA 22305
  (703) 519-3846
  www.eangus.org
  e-mail: eangus@eangus.org

- **National Guard Association of the United States**
  1 Massachusetts Avenue, NW
  Washington, DC 20001
  (202) 789-0031
  Fax: (202) 682-9358
  www.ngaus.org

- **Army Reserve Headquarters Hotline**
  (800) 359-8483 ext. 464-8995/8947

- **National Guard Family Programs Office**
  To inquire about your state's Family Program Coordinator, contact:
  National Volunteer Coordinator
  6848 S. Revere Parkway
  Englewood, CO 80112-6709
  (303) 397-3034

DSN 877-2034
Commercial fax (303) 397-3003
DSN fax 877-2003

* *You Belong to the National Guard Family*
Available from your Family Support Center, your chaplain, or
the publisher:
Scriptographic Booklets
Channing L. Bete Co. Inc.
200 State Road
South Deerfield, MA 01373-0200
(800) 477-4776
e-mail: custsvcs@channing-bete.com
www.channing-bete.com

Appendix

Acronyms

ACS	Army Community Services
AER	Army Emergency Relief
AFB	Air Force Base
AFHA	Armed Forces Hostess Association
AFTB	Army Family Team Building
ANG	Air National Guard
ARNG	Army National Guard
ATM	Automatic Teller Machine
BX	Base Exchange
CACO	Casualty Assistance Calls Officer
CAO	Casualty Assistance Officer
CHAMPUS	Civilian Health and Medical Program of the Uniformed Services
CHAMPVA	Civilian Health and Medical Program of the Department of Veterans Affairs
CNO	Chief of Naval Operations
CNT	Casualty Notification Team
CO	Commanding Officer
COMSEC	Communications Security
CREDO	Chaplains Religious Development Operation

DACOWITS	Defense Advisory Committee on Women in the Services
DEERS	Defense Enrollment Eligibility Reporting System
DOD	Department of Defense
DPP	Deferred Payment Plan
DSN	Defense Switched Network
FLCL	Family Life Communication Line
FSC	Family Support Center or Family Service Center
HQ	Headquarters
ID	Identification
IG	Inspector General
ITT	Information, Tickets, and Tours
JTF	Joint Task Force
KVN	Key Volunteer Network
LES	Leave and Earnings Statement
MAPsite	Military Assistance Program Site
MARS	Military Affiliated Radio System
MCFTB	Marine Corps Family Team Building
MIA	Missing in Action
MOPS	Mothers of Preschoolers
MP	Military Police
MPSM	Military Personnel Support Ministry
NCESGR	National Committee for Employer Support of the Guard and Reserve
NCO	Non-Commissioned Officer
NMFA	National Military Family Association
NWCA	Navy Wives Clubs of America
OCF	Officer's Christian Fellowship
ODS	Operation Desert Shield/Storm
OPSEC	Operations Security
PCS	Permanent Change of Station
POA	Power of Attorney
POV	Privately Owned Vehicle
POW	Prisoner of War
PRIMUS	Primary Care for the Uniformed Services
PX	Post Exchange

SAC	Strategic Air Command
SATO	Scheduled Airline Ticket Office
SF	Security Forces (formerly Security Police)
SSN	Social Security Number
TAPS	Tragedy Assistance Program for Survivors
TMO	Traffic Management Office
TSP	Thrift Savings Plan
USA	United States Army
USAF	United States Air Force
USAR	United States Army Reserve
USAREUR	United States Army in Europe
USO	United Service Organization
USERRA	Uniformed Services Employment and Reemployment Rights Act

To order additional copies of

WHEN DUTY CALLS

Have your credit card ready and call

Toll free: (877) 421-READ (7323)

or send $14.99* each plus $5.95 S&H** to

WinePress Publishing
PO Box 428
Enumclaw, WA 98022

www.winepresspub.com

*WA residents, add 8.4% sales tax

**add $1.50 S&H for each additional book ordered